MINDFULNESS WORKBOOK FOR TEEN ANXIETY

MINDFULNESS WORKBOOK FOR

teen anxiety

Engaging Mindfulness Exercises to Manage Your Worries and Find Relief

SALLY ANNJANECE STEVENS, LCSW

ROCKRIDGE PRESS

Interior and Cover Designer: Angela Navarra
Art Producer: Hannah Dickerson
Editor: Kelly Koester

All images used under license lisa_kalev/ Creative Market. Author photo courtesy of Jessica McKimmey.

ISBN: Print 978-1-63807-349-9
eBook 978-1-63807-809-8

R0

Thank you for those who stood behind me, pushing me to the front, challenging me to be creative and speak up. Your investment has paid it forward. Thank you to my colleagues who cheered me on and my family for always letting the light in (Nathan, Kirin, & Finnley)!

CONTENTS

INTRODUCTION

My name is Sally Stevens, and I am a licensed clinical social worker and school mental health administrator; I was a school social worker for more than a decade, working with teenagers most of my career. I am also a really awesome sister (that's what I tell my brothers and sisters anyway), a wife, and mother to a talented daughter and son. Mental health and education are my passions, and I think anxiety and mindfulness can be used as key tools to challenge and inspire you to be the best version of yourself.

Anxiety forces you to rise to the occasion to accept the challenge at hand; mindfulness is the key to success by keeping you focused and steady. It is likely that you find anxiety impacting your daily interactions with the people in your life. After much personal and professional work, I am a ninja at managing anxiety, but it has taken time and energy to embrace anxiety as an instrument in my life. Embracing anxiety as an instrument of success has reframed the negative messages around mental health for me. Using mindfulness has centered my awareness and supported my focus. Mindfulness has helped my students, my therapeutic practice, and me. I hope this workbook will provide that for you, too.

Cheers for reading and participating in this workbook! Whether someone who cares about you recommended this book or you found it yourself to support you and help you better understand your anxiety, you are where you are supposed to be. Together we will take the path ahead one step at a time, at a pace that supports you moving forward day by day, by developing a sense of reflection and awareness. Like any struggle, when you understand it more, you gain the wisdom to make powerful changes.

This workbook will help guide you throughout nine chapters; each chapter is geared to build on to the next. First, you are going to learn about anxiety and how to harness mindfulness to develop awareness of how anxiety is impacting your life and your relationships. You will cultivate self-compassion and give yourself permission to release judgment. You will embrace anxiety as part of yourself, opening yourself up for acceptance and self-love. Through self-love and self-compassion, you will begin to trust yourself and your emotions. Lastly, you will let go of regret, judgment, and shame and embrace the best version of yourself. You know, the perfectly imperfect version who developed self-awareness and decided to challenge themselves to be mentally stronger through mindfulness!

This workbook is a practical guide of mindfulness. Using the seven foundational attitudes developed by mindfulness master Jon Kabat-Zinn, you will learn how to use a beginner's mind, opening yourself to embrace non-judging. Once you have learned to release judging yourself and others, you will move to embrace acceptance. Acceptance will help you cultivate patience, and through patience you will learn to trust yourself and others in your life. Once you have developed trust and patience, you will move forward to non-striving. Lastly, you will learn the power of letting go.

Each chapter will help you evaluate the storm that anxiety can cause and help shine light into the resilience that you have developed because your brain has been challenged by it. Stress and anxiety are normal components of basic living. You likely tend to avoid pain and distance yourself through escape and avoidance. Sometimes you may develop habits that hinder you from going forward. Each chapter and exercise within this workbook will support you building moment-to-moment awareness. You will use the methods outlined in each chapter to help manage anxiety when it is negatively impacting your life, taking a step forward with each and every exercise, each and every page. Your focus on each mindfulness attitude will help you develop a new sense of wisdom. Your perspective will widen using mindfulness; you will discover how you see situations and relationships and how anxiety has impacted your abilities and possibilities. Mindfulness will bring an enhanced quality of life, shifting you from fear to focusing on the present moment so you can enjoy your life minute by minute.

CHAPTER ONE

THE MINDFULNESS AND ANXIETY CONNECTION

Welcome to the first step forward in managing your anxiety with mindfulness. As the Buddhist teacher and author Frank Ostaseski said, "Your thoughts and emotions are not who you are. They pass through you, but they are not you." It is important to remember that anxiety does not define you, and making the commitment to this workbook is a big and brave step. Your effort to make small changes through the reading and completion of the various exercises in this workbook will improve your ability to achieve long-lasting personal growth and be the best version of yourself.

WHY CHOOSE MINDFULNESS?

Celebrities from Beyoncé to LeBron James have been open about how practicing mindfulness has improved their game, reduced their anxiety, and enhanced their energy. Mindfulness has become a go-to for wellness and health in large part because it's a mental superpower! It is the ability to have full awareness of what is going on in your head, moment-by-moment, scene-by-scene without judgment. Through mindfulness, you can become more aware and present in your feelings, thoughts, physical sensations, and responses without reacting blindly or automatically to stresses, worries, or challenges. What's better is that this mental superpower can become a new normalcy; without the interruption of your brain, your senses are actually very receptive and curious about your environments through lenses that don't categorize things as right or wrong. When you choose mindfulness, you can tap into limitless levels of empathy and compassion for yourself and your anxiety.

The Pillars of Mindfulness

While you may not be familiar with him or his work, professor and writer Jon Kabat-Zinn has helped people of all ages and walks of life understand mindfulness. He is often referred to as the "master of mindfulness." Through his considerable time and work within the field, he has identified nine key foundational attitudes for developing mindfulness as a practice. In this book, the primary focus will be on the original seven essential attitudes, from which you will work to build a foundation. Gratitude and generosity were later added to the original seven that Kabat-Zinn had identified, and throughout the workbook, these will be lightly touched on as well.

1. **Beginner's Mind:** You open yourself to view your life through a new lens. Imagine you've been wearing glasses with fingerprints all over them for a long time, and someone cleaned your glasses, enabling you to see your world clearly. You can finally see sharp outlines,

vibrant colors, unique shapes and textures, and lively details. Fresh eyes help you let go of your assumptions and judgments, transforming you into a learner. A beginner's mind is a positive, because you're more open to learning and the possibilities are infinite; conversely, when you look at the world as an "expert," there is very little to learn or see without a fresh perspective.

2. **Non-Judging:** Every day your brain sorts people, things, and events into categories based on how they make you feel—good, bad, and indifferent. Your brain makes snap judgments, labeling things subconsciously based on how you value them. From this you develop robotic reactions without awareness. To stop boxing and labeling, you need to become aware of your biases and blind spots. To pay closer attention to your thoughts, you need to pay attention to how you filter your thinking. If you see things only through your likes and dislikes, you have already boxed and labeled everything. When you break this habit, you can live more authentically.

3. **Acceptance**: You need to be willing to see things how they are in the moment, taking something for what it is. You may not always like what it is, but you need to see the truth and open yourself to recognize the present stage you are at. It is a path to release the demands you put on yourself and focus on the facts of the world and your own life. Acceptance helps you love the person in the mirror today, and at every stage of life when you look at your reflection. When you open yourself to see your feelings, your thoughts, your ideas, and your biases, it unlocks the door to change and sustains growth.

4. **Patience:** Your life and brain have become accustomed to instant gratification because information is so readily available through technology (Instagram, TikTok, Google, etc.). Developing patience means embracing the idea that things will happen in their own time. Life is a process, and looking for shortcuts or racing to the future can create anxiety and stress. When your thoughts wander too far ahead, you need to develop awareness to be comfortable in

the moment. It is important to find joy in the process. When you are able to step back and stay in the moment, you encourage yourself to learn each step of the way.

5. **Trust:** Nurturing your sense of internal trust will help you become authentic and honest with yourself. You need to be mindful and pay attention to when you feel vulnerable emotionally. When you don't trust yourself, you might have feelings of confusion, helplessness, or hopelessness. Trust allows you to seek answers within, versus going outside yourself and depending on others' feelings or actions. Trust helps you take responsibility when you make a mistake and allows you to hold yourself accountable for your choices. Learning to be mindful, honest, and trusting strengthens your ability to stay curious and nonjudgmental. Trust from within helps you build trust in others.

6. **Non-Striving:** As a student, you likely set goals for most of your efforts, such as getting good grades. Non-striving is the opposite of goal-setting; it is effectively mindful non-doing. With non-striving you let go of the idea and pressures of a finish line. Sometimes your brain tells you that you are not enough, that you need to be more. When you strive for more, it sends the message that something is wrong, that you need to be someone better, someone else. Setting intentions is part of mindfulness, but non-striving is a way for you to view yourself without judgment and helps you see things the way they are. It is okay to not be okay all the time.

7. **Letting Go:** Your thoughts, feelings, and memories all follow patterns, much like your brain. Sometimes you try to control these patterns, or else you get stuck in the same cycle. That cycle can be like a heavy cloud over you and cause stress and anxiety. You need to be open to letting thoughts, feelings, and experiences go, not unlike the experience of falling asleep. Before bed you may tell your brain "it is time to be free of all the worry and focus on rest." You can take the same approach into your waking hours and tell your brain to let go of heavy feelings and focus on the present.

Through this workbook, you are going to learn how these seven attitudes can positively impact your life one step at a time. Each chapter of this book will embrace these foundational attitudes and provide strategies and exercises to develop tools for your brain's toolbox to help you manage your anxiety.

Mindfully Manage Your Anxiety

Your brain is wired to protect you from anything that it perceives as threatening. In your daily life, your brain mindlessly thin-slices, making very quick assumptions and judgments with small amounts of information and narrowly categorizing situations, people, and events. If your brain thinks there is a shark, it will go into fight-flight-freeze as a protective response. You will amp up to respond to the shark, either kicking it, swimming away, or playing dead to survive. Unfortunately, your thoughts can sometimes be inaccurate or not necessarily rooted in reality; these are called cognitive distortions. Think of it this way: Your brain draws the picture of a situation, such as being in the ocean and hearing a sound, and adaptively reacts with anxiety. "It must be a shark, and it is going to eat me!" If you could acknowledge the distortions in your brain and how you are making snap judgments, you would be aware of the present moment and the reality of the situation, that it's unlikely an actual shark, but rather a harmless dolphin splashing around in the water.

Mindfulness is the tool that helps you develop more awareness and encourages you to avoid reacting from a place of anxiety. When you spend mental energy boxing and labeling thoughts, feelings, ideas, and events, it is the equivalent of cognitive labor. Think of it like a conveyor belt that's moving so fast, you're barely able to take in what it's carrying, but just watching it makes you dizzy. Mindfulness helps the conveyor belt slow down, if not stop altogether, and allows you to see clearly what's before you, perhaps even appreciating it for what it is. Staying present and seeing things objectively improves your brain's problem-solving skills as you redistribute the cognitive energy more efficiently into a positive result.

ANXIETY DOESN'T DEFINE YOU

Anxiety is an alarm system installed in your brain for free, no monthly subscription required. When your brain perceives harm, danger, or threat, the alarm system goes off. Your brain and your body immediately react to the alarm system, causing a change in your thoughts, feelings, behaviors, and physiological attributes, such as heart rate, body temperature, and breathing. Symptoms of anxiety can be unique from person to person—how you experience anxiety may be different from how a friend experiences anxiety.

Anxiety is a mental health disorder that impacts nearly one in three adolescents ages 13 to 18, according to the National Institute of Mental Health (NIMH). That means for every three friends you have, one of them is experiencing thoughts of worry more days than not for at least six months. There are many reasons why anxiety is so widespread: familial and peer pressure, school violence, media exposure, and the demands of technology and social media, on top of ever-growing expectations for students. You are not alone in experiencing anxiety or wanting to learn how to identify it and develop skills and tools to better manage it. Experiencing anxiety does not mean you are flawed; rather, it means you are human. If you are struggling to manage your anxiety, I have great news! This workbook will help you develop a personal plan that fits into your schedule and puts your brain on the track to success!

Feelings

Anxiety changes your emotions and your feelings by causing an irrational fear of something—a perceived threat or danger. You might feel nervousness and restlessness, which make your body tense. Anxiety can make you feel weak, tired, agitated, irritable, and panicky. You may feel dread about engaging with others or feel a lack of energy in taking action. You may rationalize avoiding situations or people because of the discomfort of the feelings. Anxiety can stir up feelings of shame, guilt, and self-judgment. Often, you may become frustrated due to feeling like you're struggling to manage the symptoms that are manifesting, especially if they are affecting your daily life. Your feelings can impact your thoughts. When you feel anxious, your thoughts become fear based, which can lead to behavior changes and physical symptoms. Feeling and emotional identification are the ticket to making changes. Once you can identify what feelings are coming up, you can effectively plan to address them.

Thoughts

Anxiety can change the way you think. It can turn your thoughts into distortions where you are not able to see things clearly. Those thoughts can become weapons against you and your relationships with others. Anxious thoughts can develop into unhelpful patterns such as spiraling. Spiraling is like a relay race where one negative thought leads to another negative thought, and to another negative thought, and so on and so on. It can take you to a dark scary hole that feels endless. Because anxiety convinces your brain that it needs to concentrate on preparing for a threat, it can cloud your ability to focus and think clearly. That cloud can rain on your thoughts, making it hard to think of anything else other than your worries. Thoughts can become obsessive in nature, too, where it feels like you are stuck between point A and point B. It is important to build awareness of how anxiety affects your thoughts and thought patterns in order to know what you need to successfully move forward.

Physical Symptoms

Anxiety can trigger your fight-flight-freeze response, causing related physical symptoms to impact your body. When adrenaline kicks in (the "fight" response), your heart rate and breathing can increase in frequency because your body feels like it needs more oxygen. Sometimes you can have a temperature reaction where you feel hot, sweaty, or even tingly. Your body is gearing up for survival. You may notice muscles tightening in your stomach, shoulders, or jaw (clenching your jaw or grinding your teeth).

Feeling restless and fidgety, like you need to move around (leg or hands shake) may also ensue, as can tension headaches and various aches and pains. Anxiety can cause insomnia, restless sleep, and interrupted sleep. (Interrupted sleep can cause other health impairments and mess with your overall mood.)

Behaviors

When your brain senses danger, anxiety is an adaptive response that feels like an appropriate method of coping in that moment. Defense mechanisms protect your brain from anxiety as a method of control. You may rub your hand over something soft, tap your nails, play with your hair, bite your nails, or shake your leg. The behaviors can become repetitive in nature and you may exhibit them without being cognizant of doing so. Anxiety can lead to safety behaviors that help you feel like you are in control in the moment. Daydreaming or disassociating from a situation is when you hide in your head and are not present in the reality of a situation. This action is referred to as escaping. Avoidance is another escapism behavior that happens when you try to evade hard feelings or emotions, a situation, an interaction, or an event.

ANXIETY TREATMENT

Mental health professionals support anxiety treatment with talk therapy. Talk therapy is the same as psychotherapy, where a mental health professional communicates one-on-one with their clients to help identify the issues that negatively impact their life and cause emotional stress. Therapists use evidence-based practices; these methods, such as cognitive behavioral therapy (CBT), have been researched to help people develop tools for their toolbox. CBT is one of the most common practices to support managing your anxiety because it helps identify the pathways in which your thoughts are developed and the patterns your thoughts follow, which ultimately lead to your behaviors. Mindfulness-based cognitive therapy helps train your thoughts to be present and resist reacting to a situation automatically, so observation can ensue. This allows you to see things clearly without preliminary snap judgments and reactions.

Getting help and treatment for anxiety is important. There are many resources on the internet, in your community, and at your school. Asking a trusted adult to support you in the process is key. If you have insurance that covers mental health, your insurer is an excellent place to start for a reference to someone local to speak with. Talk therapy can also be virtual through telehealth or a convenient video chat for a confidential session, similar to FaceTime or Google Meet. Additionally, your doctor or a psychiatrist can prescribe medication, if necessary. Depending on one's level of anxiety, the combination of medication and talk therapy may be the most successful treatment.

Calm & Safety

Throughout this workbook, reading about anxiety, whether it's the science behind it or the feelings it produces, may trigger your own feelings of anxiety. It is important for you to know that that's perfectly normal. If that happens, I encourage you to use the following supportive self-touch technique to feel calm and/or safe:

1. Place your left or right hand over your heart and below your collarbone (like you would when saying the Pledge of Allegiance).
2. Feel the comforting weight of your hand on your chest.
3. You can also tap your hand or move it in circles to cultivate a sense of calm and safety, as physical touch releases oxytocin, a hormone that reduces stress and anxiety.

HOW TO USE THIS WORKBOOK

If you are feeling anxious, know that you are not alone! According to Our World in Data (2018), 284 million people in the world live with a diagnosis of anxiety. That means that 284 million people were able to seek help and find assistance; but considering there are 8 billion people living on the planet, that suggests many are still needing help. By choosing this workbook, you are taking a step toward seeking and finding assistance.

Throughout this workbook you will learn the characteristics of anxiety and how it impacts your life. Each of the nine chapters will focus on a foundational mindfulness attitude to support your personal growth and self-development. You will see multiple mindfulness activities and exercises to support overcoming the impact of anxiety, from symptom reduction to long-term management. The goal is that after reading and engaging with this workbook, you will feel confident using the tools you need to improve your life one mindfulness exercise at a time. Just like lifting weights strengthens your body, you are going to exercise in a way that strengthens your brain. If you'd like, share with a friend that you're embarking upon this journey; mental wellness is the key to a healthy balanced life and successful relationships.

As you move through this workbook, remember that you know yourself best and what resonates with you the most. This book is not chronological, so feel free to jump around to sections that you feel drawn to, or to skip over sections that don't feel as relevant to you but that you may want to come back to later. Be mindful of your capacity (what you can take in) and openness in the moment (what you are willing to receive). There is no one-size-fits-all approach for self-growth; the path is unique for everyone. If you are drawn to something else, honor yourself and your judgment, and acknowledge what works best for you. My hope for you is that completing this workbook will benefit your journey of self-reflection, mindfulness, and personal growth. Even if things can feel challenging at times, know that the investment is worth the journey.

Finally, this workbook is meant to be a tool and not to replace any other treatment you may be engaged in, such as talk therapy or medication. In fact, you may find that this workbook is a wonderful tool to use in tandem with your current plan. Whatever the case may be, this workbook will give you that much more support in investing in your sense of well-being. When you come across exercises and ideas that you find most helpful, you may want to mark the pages to revisit them again at another time. And feel free to take a picture of the positive affirmations throughout to have a mental boost on the go!

YOU'VE GOT THIS!

Anxiety can make you feel uncomfortable. It can change the way you feel, think, and behave. It can also affect your physiology. But even when this is the case, you are still in charge of your mind and body. Take a moment and repeat the following:

"I am my own captain."

"I steer my ship in the direction I choose."

"Discomfort challenges me to be the best version of myself."

"Today, I am the best version of myself I can be."

BEFORE YOU BEGIN

Life is full of challenges and hardships, which can sometimes feel like storms of emotions. Some of these storms are filled with lightning and rain, whereas others bring about only a light drizzle. The upside is that storms prove the strength of your anchors, or the people, things, and ideas that help you stay grounded and healthy. Anxiety may be the storm that shows up as a drizzle (barely anxious) on some days and as lightning and hail (a panic attack) on other days. It can also be anything in between. No matter how anxiety feels, working on your mental health is the best investment you can make in your life. There are various ways to invest, and the frequency of that effort can be anything from daily to a few times a week. Throughout this workbook there will be exercises to confront where you may feel emotionally and cognitively spent. When you are working toward mental wellness, you are pushing yourself to be the best version of you; this takes hard work, dedication, and resilience. Without a little struggle, the journey would be easy, but the growth would be minimal. I cannot promise results; however, I can tell you that you are worth the time and energy of the quest to manage your anxiety through mindfulness.

Throughout this personal quest, I ask that you honor yourself, acknowledge your feelings, and be aware of your body. Negative feelings and pain can ricochet, and often you may cope with them in unhealthy ways, such as hiding, stuffing them down with avoidance, or projecting them elsewhere. Looking inside yourself can feel uncomfortable. Make the commitment to challenge yourself to get comfortable with being uncomfortable. Set aside 10 to 15 minutes a day on your calendar/phone and commit to this workbook. If you need to skip a day, that's okay—take the time for yourself and recharge without shame or judgment. If you fall during the journey, dust off your knees and pick up where you left off. When you are ready to make changes in your life, this workbook will be here. You will weather the storm and chart yourself a new voyage, where anxiety does not wear the captain's hat! Congratulations on finishing chapter 1—you are ready to set sail!

POSITIVE VIBES

Today marks the moment that you have decided anxiety will not be the loudest voice in your brain. You have decided to take the mindful path forward. Mental wellness is key to living a balanced life, and honoring yourself and your journey is the first step forward!

YOUR TAKEAWAYS

*"Start where you are. Use what you have.
Do what you can."*

— Arthur Ashe

→ You learned about the power of mindfulness and its benefits for treating anxiety.

→ You learned about mindfulness's seven foundational attitudes: beginner's mind, non-judging, acceptance, patience, trust, non-striving, and letting go.

→ You understand how anxiety can affect your thoughts, feelings, behaviors, and your physical body, but that it does not define you!

→ You learned about the various methods of treatment for anxiety such as talk therapy, cognitive-behavioral therapy, mindfulness-based cognitive therapy, and medication.

→ You learned how supportive self-touch can reduce stress and anxiety by relieving adrenaline and oxytocin in your body.

→ Modeling help-seeking for others may also help someone in your life get the help they need.

CHAPTER TWO

SEE THINGS AS THEY ARE

Even though your mind may often get stuck on seeing things as you have always seen them, remember that if nothing else, today, this moment right now, is new. You have never read these words before, the way you are reading them now, and that alone is an opportunity to see things in a new way and to experience new feelings. In this chapter, you will learn how to develop a beginner's mind by observing your world and yourself with fresh eyes, thereby freeing yourself from previous assumptions, attitudes, beliefs, ideas, and desires. Go through this chapter as a learner and researcher, someone in the first steps of observing, without yet having created a hypothesis. Focus on seeing everything for the first time and open yourself up to each new learning opportunity and to each moment. One great way to get started is to settle down in a room where you feel safe, comfortable, and secure; this will allow your fresh perspective and open mind to thrive.

THE MINDFUL WAY

The practice of mindfulness combined with the principle of a beginner's mind helps you look at circumstances in your life with fresh eyes and take a learner's approach. Instead of looking at things as if you completely know how they work and what they are, with nothing new to learn, you can ask curious and helpful questions like, *"How does this work?"* To develop a beginner's mind, you need to shift your expectations and throw out your assumptions. If you can take a learner's approach to life, without shaming yourself for making any mistakes, your anxiety will lessen. Mistakes aren't failures, they're new opportunities for reflection and learning.

Think of an idea that lives inside a box. If the idea is closed in by the four walls of the box, it has very little room to grow or evolve into anything else. When you let go of your assumptions and expectations, you allow the restrictive sides of the box around them to fall away and open yourself up to new possibilities. You begin to see things with a renewed sense of awe and inquiry. Picture something you have never eaten before but are about to try for the first time. You look at the color(s); you attempt to make connections to things you have eaten previously or that probably tasted similar; you investigate its texture; you look at it with wonder because you've never eaten it before. All the possibilities are ready for you to explore. If you assumed you knew what it tasted like, and how much you'd enjoy eating it, you'd put it in the box. Your goal is to stay out of the box!

If I asked what the color of an apple is, you'd probably say "red" or "green" if you thought I was referring to the fruit. If you thought I was referring to technology, like the company Apple, you'd probably say "white." Color is a matter of perception and subjective interpretation, something that is drawn from previous experiences and places of reference, to assist you in identifying and categorizing what you are viewing. Now, take that "apple" and rename it "anxiety." Anxiety may look slightly different depending on who you ask, but the shape and symptoms share the same theme: fear. Anxiety is your brain being triggered by the anticipation of fear, and, left unmanaged, it can even take over as the captain of your ship.

In kindergarten, I remember being asked what I wanted to "bee" when I grew up while making yellow-and-black construction-paper bees. That bee could only be one thing—a teacher, firefighter, singer, or doctor. What I was never told was I could "bee more than one thing." Donald Glover defied that project when he grew up; he bee-came an actor, singer, rapper, comedian, writer, producer, and director. You may know him as Childish Gambino; his five Grammy Awards, two Golden Globe Awards, and two Emmy Awards threw out life's expectations to be one thing. Glover said, "If it makes you nervous . . . you're doing it right." Like Glover, let yourself use fresh eyes, develop questions eagerly, and let go of your assumptions by staying present and being open to the endless possibilities. Your nervousness, fear, and anxiety will be transformed as you cultivate your beginner's mind.

COMMON ANXIETY PATTERNS

Your thoughts become patterns that you can trace, just like in a connect-the-dots picture. Anxiety has a pattern of twisting your thoughts into distortions that cause you to perceive reality inaccurately. Think of 3D glasses. They're perfect for seeing that new blockbuster with special effects in theaters, but if you wore them outside the theater while going about a normal day, you would see everything through a red-and-blue filter, rather than in true color. Distortions block a beginner's mindset because they prevent you from seeing things as they are, without judgment or misconception. In this section, we are going to look at two cognitive distortions that can prevent your beginner's mind from developing: overgeneralization and should-statements.

Overgeneralization

Overgeneralization is when you take one event or situation and make a general conclusion. That "truth" you come up with guides your thought patterns in life. For example, imagine that you gave a presentation in class last month and received a low grade. This week you have a presentation for another class, and you automatically tell yourself that you will also get a low grade because of the result from last time. Your thoughts have turned on you and tell you that you aren't good at giving presentations, you will never be, and you deserve a low grade. In this scenario, there is no room for growth and no room for learning because you have painted a picture about what will *always* happen. If you use your beginner's mind, however, you can leave last month's presentation in the past, along with the negative feelings that try to tell you that you're not enough. Your beginner's mind can also help you take the new presentation step by step, day by day, without judgment or fear, with confidence and trust.

Should-Statements

Should-statements—which can also take the form of "must," "ought," and "have to"—are another thought process that attempts to box you in. Also referred to as imperative statements (constraints, requirements, commands), should-statements criticize yourself and others for behavior, thoughts, and feelings. They transform into a set of made-up rules you have created in your head that emotionally punish you through shame and guilt. Say, for example, that you did not do well on a recent test. Your thoughts may say to you, "You *should* have studied more, you *have to* study every day, you *ought to* have known you would do badly." Should-statements tell you that you are not enough (which isn't true), or you knew better than how you behaved (which isn't a fair assessment), and leave you feeling guilt and shame for not measuring up to the rigid, demanding rules you created in your own mind. Should-statements assume an expert mind rather than a beginner's, leaving very little room for possibility. You cannot stay present and see each moment for what it is if you believe you know the outcome or route you should have taken.

Take comfort knowing that each day is a brand-new moment in your life. Many authors have referred to the present as a gift; lean into taking your "present" and open it with curiosity. Negative thought patterns and worries can take away from your opportunity for growth, and thoughts of worry can box you in or keep you stuck on a loop, but what about taking in each moment without an idea of what is happening next and welcoming it as a brand-new experience? Your personal forecast will shift from cloudy skies, and instead brightly open up with possibilities of what is yet to come.

REAL TALK

Olivia used to stuff her feelings down and would do anything and everything not to acknowledge them. She would tell herself over and over again that she was fine, even though her neck and face were fiery red. Eventually, Olivia would feel overwhelmed by her feelings and break down crying.

We had been practicing a powerful phrase together for the last two weeks: "It's okay not to be okay." Sometimes, we need permission to do hard things; feeling feelings can be a hard undertaking. That day, Olivia came into my office annoyed and said, "Feeling my feelings sucks!" I laughed and said, "That means you are aware of them, which is a total win!" Olivia sat down and grabbed a pillow to hug it. "I was doing all these things and avoiding my anxiety and now that I am working on learning things, it's everywhere! I go to class—hello, anxiety! Sitting next to me—oh, hello, it's anxiety! Taking a test—hello again, anxiety here! I squeeze my pencil so tight, my hand hurts! When Michael asked me for help, my words got stuck in my throat and I stuttered. While I'm reading in class, my leg is constantly shaking. It's super annoying!"

Even though she felt so worked up, I was smiling on the inside, because Olivia was using an open mind; previously, she had not been as aware of her anxiety as she was now. She was paying attention and seeing clearly how anxiety would come up throughout her day and in several situations. I told her, "I am really proud of you. Feeling your feelings is tough and can be exhausting. Stuffing them down works for the moment, but unfortunately they usually just come back louder and stronger." The goal was for Olivia to allow herself to slow down and feel her feelings.

Sometimes you move through your days and thoughts and emotions quickly so that your feelings don't have the opportunity to catch up, which keeps them quiet. Anxiety can also propel you to move fast because you are feeling pure adrenaline in your body. A beginner's mind allows you to stop running the anxiety sprint. You can instead sign up to run a marathon and look at your behaviors as you see them for the first time, mile marker by mile marker. By acknowledging your anxiety and seeing clearly how it impacts your day, you can decide to manage it through mindfulness. The beginner's mind provides you insight into what you really need. Stay brave and use your beginner's mind; you will continually learn something different and empowering about yourself.

Five Senses Grounding

Your body has the gift of five senses: sight, touch, hearing, smell, and taste. Most of the time you use your senses unconsciously; the sensing organs in your body send messages to your brain, helping you process, comprehend, and perceive the world around you. Your senses can also help your brain become that much more grounded, which brings attention to what is going on around you and keeps you feeling balanced. When you are grounded and aware, you are able to support yourself with a calm mind and react to life's situations with self-control.

Let's get grounded!

1. Breathe in and hold for 3 counts (1, 2, 3) and breathe out and hold for 3 counts (1, 2, 3).
2. Repeat two or three times to establish a clean slate for your beginner's mind and help open up your five senses.

Sight: What are three things you see around you that bring you joy?
Example: "I see my dog chewing on a toy, a tree outside my window, and my funny little brother."

Touch: What are three things you can feel?
Example: "I can feel my legs crossed in a chair, my hair on my shoulders, and my sweatshirt keeping me warm."

Hearing: What are three things you can hear?
Example: "I can hear music playing, a bird chirping outside, and my refrigerator humming."

Smell: What are three things you can smell?
Example: "I can smell food cooking in the kitchen, a scented candle burning, and the lotion on my hands."

Taste: What are two things you can taste?
Example: "I can taste the gum in my mouth and the honey in my tea."

Reality Check

With an open mind, you are able to see things that much more clearly. Anxiety can feel like blurred vision, where you can't see 100 percent of the shapes, colors, and details. Just like when you go to the eye doctor to check if your vision is 20/20, let's measure if your anxiety is 20/20. In order to measure anxiety, you need to evaluate three things: frequency (how often), duration (how long), and intensity (level of stress).

Keep your beginner's mind eyeglasses on as you take this 10-question quiz. The goal is to answer the questions honestly so that you may learn something new. Think of the last two weeks and how you were feeling when you answer the questions without judgment. Mark your frequency selection in the boxes with a check, a star, or an X. Simply observe the answers that come to mind—no need to analyze them.

QUESTION	ALWAYS	OFTEN	SOMETIMES	RARELY	NEVER
I worry about a lot of different things.					
I am easily annoyed or grouchy.					
It is hard for me to relax.					
I feel nervous, anxious, or impatient.					
I am afraid something bad will happen.					
It is hard for me to sit still without fidgeting.					
I cannot control my worried thoughts.					
I have a hard time focusing and feel distracted.					

QUESTION	ALWAYS	OFTEN	SOMETIMES	RARELY	NEVER
I have a hard time getting to sleep or staying asleep.					
I avoid doing things that make me nervous.					

Reflect: Hopefully, you are able to see how your anxiety is impacting your day and life with open eyes. If you logged most of your answers on the left (always), you can use mindfulness to eventually move your answers more toward the right (never).

Out of the Box

To truly have a beginner's mindset and stay out of any rigid or limiting boxes pertaining to how you think and feel, you need to stay curious and let go of assumptions, expectations, and judgments. You need to give yourself permission not to have the answers, but rather to create the questions. What do you need to let go of? Maybe it's the stress of who you think you are supposed to be, how many followers you should have, or what achievements you should have by now.

What three things do you need to let go of in order to adopt a beginner's mind?

_____

_____

_____

For two minutes, journal about why you need to accept imagination and inquiry as a practice and how it will benefit you.

_____

_____

_____

_____

_____

_____

That's My Jam

Think of your favorite song. Once you identify it, if possible, find it on YouTube, Spotify, Apple, or Amazon. You can even consider finding an instrumental version without the lyrics if you want to challenge yourself.

Before you hit Play, think back to your anxiety quiz results and where you are at in this moment. With that in mind, hit Play on your favorite song and listen like it is the first time you have ever heard it. Notice each note, each instrument, each word. If your mind drifts, bring it back to listening. Try not to skip ahead of the beat or the words in your mind because you know it so well; stay with the song line by line, beat by beat. Observe how you listen to the song: Is your inner artist staying present, or are they ready for the next song on the set list?

You can use this exercise when your thoughts are getting ahead of you and you feel like you're reacting mechanically. Music helps open you up emotionally and connect you to your feelings, allowing you to stay present.

YOU'VE GOT THIS!

On your worst days, anxiety can make you feel off balance and out of control. If ever you trip and fall en route to your destination, you learn to slow down and step over the bump in the path. As rock musician and filmmaker Frank Zappa said, "A mind is like a parachute. It doesn't work if it's not open." Let's open your parachute. Only positive things will happen when you open yourself to new things, new vantage points, and new experiences.

Affirmation: *"Pull the cord, enjoy the view, I have a new perspective! I can be and do anything!"*

Inside Outside

Mindful eating has many benefits, such as weight loss, reduction of overeating, and awareness of your emotional relationship to food. When you pay attention to your eating, you're able to use all five of your senses. You are also able to observe your emotional and physical reactions to the foods you eat. If possible, for this exercise, get a lemon and cut it in half.

Using your senses and the Beginner's Mind Guide below, what do you notice about a lemon on the outside and on the inside?

BEGINNER'S MIND GUIDE:	OUTSIDE:	INSIDE:
What color(s) do you see?		
What do you taste if you lick or bite it?		
Can you hear anything?		
What do you smell?		
What does the texture feel like?		

Taking something ordinary like a lemon and focusing on what you could learn from it is a good metaphor for what it's like, and why it's great, to broaden your mind.

Your feelings may look very different to someone on the outside than how you feel them on the inside. Others may believe that you are calm and collected when on the inside you feel stressed, worried, or sad. Taking a beginner's mind approach will lessen your assumptions and create a space to be open to seeing new things for the good, bad, and everything in between.

Tech-Mate

Technology and smart devices can make the day efficient and fun, allowing you to access information and the far reaches of the world in seconds. In many ways your phone is the equivalent of your tech-best friend. These days, artificial intelligence (such as Siri, Google, and Alexa) can play the music you request, answer your questions, and even tell you stories or jokes. Your devices connect you to friends, school, celebrities, news, etc. But how often do you stop and admire the sense of curiosity they foster in your life? Technology helps you look at things with a new perspective; every time you search on the internet, you are opening your mind to learning new information. It helps shake your assumptions and what you thought you knew.

→ **Write down a list of five things you used your device(s) to search for today.**

→ Why/how did your brain spark curiosity?

→ What new detail are you seeing for the first time, with fresh eyes?

Reflection: Less than 60 percent of the world had access to the World Wide Web in January 2021. Does that statistic make you realize how much you take such an extraordinary tool for granted? Say "Thank you!" to your devices for helping your sparks of curiosity grow into fires of knowledge!

Reality Check Reflection

Using the Reality Check exercise in this chapter (page 24), let's look closer at how anxiety is impacting your life. With an open mind, think about what surprised you or about something that came up that you knew was there but didn't pay much attention to. For example, anxiety may impact your sleep more than you really realize or admit. In this exercise, reflect on what you can learn from this information and how you can now positively change your perspective.

Which of the 10 areas on the Reality Check exercise surprised you or affect you more than you realized? List all.

_____

_____

_____

When you marked the boxes, which one area sparked curiosity?

_____

_____

_____

What is something that you identified that is causing stress on a daily basis related to your answer above?

_____

_____

_____

Using a beginner's mind, what is something new that you were able to learn?

_____

_____

_____

What is one thing you need this week to help you keep your beginner's mind open to your anxiety?

_____

_____

_____

MINDFUL MOMENT

If you have a very young cousin, sister, brother, or neighbor, think about what it's like to observe them seeing something for the first time, how their eyes light up with awe and wonder. When you don't prioritize a mindful beginner's mind, your thoughts become stuck, because you leave very little room for feelings of awe or wonder. Being stuck in your own thoughts can also hurt you, because you leave little room for a different outcome. If you think something will always be a certain way, then it surely always will. It is the same for your relationships with yourself and with others. When you use your beginner's mind, you can be anything, do anything, learn anything, accomplish anything. Anything also becomes possible in relationships with others when you open yourself up, because you are able to learn new things about your family or friends. Doing so allows you to become closer, because you make space for new things, new memories, new ideas, and new feelings. You have to develop this as a habit in order for it to become a healthy and mindful pattern and avoid feeling boxed in by your anxiety, your fear, and your old beliefs. By not worrying about the outcome and not burdening yourself with the expectation to be an expert in all things, you can use that energy and time to learn and grow into the best version of yourself. That version you believe in will benefit not just yourself; it will benefit those around you, too.

POSITIVE VIBES

You can always improve your vision when you keep an open mind. A new perspective is just a gentle wave away on this voyage. If you stay brave and keep your eyes open, you'll do just fine and find yourself in an ocean of positive vibes ahead.

YOUR TAKEAWAYS

"Replace fear of the unknown with curiosity."

— Billy Cox

→ You learned that a beginner's mind keeps your mind open to new possibilities.

→ Anxiety patterns cloud your reality, and overgeneralizations and should-haves cause you to feel shame and guilt.

→ The beginner's mind provides an opportunity for learning what you really need.

→ When you open yourself up to new things, you create space for your relationships with yourself, friends, and family to grow.

→ Using your senses is a great way to get grounded and practice being open-minded.

→ Curiosity is sparked each day, and paying attention to it will help foster an enriched life.

Idea Questions

→ How will you use your beginner's mind this week?

→ When you feel yourself getting stuck on the conveyor belt of assumptions and beliefs, how will you redirect yourself and safely get off?

→ How will being open to learning new things help your relationships with friends, family, and peers?

→ What is the most surprising lesson you learned from this chapter?

CHAPTER THREE

DON'T JUDGE

Your brain can function like a judging factory; your ideas, thoughts, and experiences ride on a conveyor belt that is focused on a *Box – Label – Ship* process. Living nonjudgmentally, however, will allow you to thrive without filtering and categorizing your relationships, experiences, and, most important, yourself. Throughout this chapter, I encourage you to visualize the best version of yourself as you develop awareness of your thoughts and judgments. Understanding these judgments will help you build self-compassion and acknowledge how awesome you are. With each day, and each page, you are investing in the most important thing—you. Give yourself permission to grow, stumble, and even trip. When you trip, observe what you need to step over next time, and do so without self-shame. Praise yourself each time you take one step, or even an inch, forward!

THE MINDFUL WAY

In your daily life, you make judgments without realizing it. When you judge something as likeable, you put it in a "like" box and store it somewhere that represents good judgments. You stack the boxes you like and seek out more of that type. If you make judgments that put something in a box labeled "bad," "not good enough," or "flawed," you discard those boxes to rid yourself of the thoughts and feelings contained within them. This automatic act of judging creates a filter through which you see your life as good, bad, or indifferent. Social media is a great example of this type of conveyor-belt style of judging. You may post what you like, or think will be liked, but are not as willing to post what seems embarrassing, uninteresting, or imperfect. If you swipe through content that you do not care about, you intentionally don't offer up hearts, emojis, or comments. Your opinions and ideas exist within a space of "I like it," "I hate it," or "I don't care." Unfortunately, your filters create biases based on those "like" and "dislike" judgments. Not unlike the video suggestions that you encounter on YouTube, your biases function as your own personal algorithm, which exposes you to the same types of thoughts and feelings and prevents you from encountering new ones.

Everyone has an anxiety bias of some kind, whether it's public speaking, eating in front of people, or having a fight with a friend. Anxiety determines your fears as well as your perception of how scary the world can be, and in turn you believe it. What's worse is when it feels like your negative thoughts judge you or make you worry that you will be judged by others. You may tell yourself you cannot do hard tasks because you have already made the judgment that it is too intimidating or too scary. By realizing that you are thinking in black and white, you can see clearly that you are looking at your world, and at yourself, through a filter. When you identify a filter, you are better equipped to remove it and begin to see reality, without the bias; you can stop labeling each idea, thought, or experience. It takes a lot of energy to power the filters through which you see the world, so let's instead channel that energy into practicing mindfulness and releasing the pressure of judgmental thoughts.

By developing awareness and staying present without judgment, you can slow down the conveyor belt through the practice of mindfulness. Mindfulness is the key to breaking free of those biases and building awareness that you make decisions robotically. Remember how the master of mindfulness, Jon Kabat-Zinn, defines mindfulness itself: "Mindfulness means paying attention in a particular way: on purpose, in the present moment, and non-judgmentally." Throughout this chapter, each exercise will help you better understand your judgments so you can revise them to better serve you rather than serving your anxiety. Living nonjudgmentally leaves less opportunity for anxiety to create judgmental reactions and more room for your inner wisdom to grow.

COMMON ANXIETY PATTERNS

Your conveyor belt of judgment creates two common cognitive distortions: (1) all-or-nothing thinking, also known as black-and-white thinking, and (2) labeling. Both distortions can negatively impact your relationship with yourself and with others. Thinking about things in extremes limits your ability to see the various colors of the rainbow in your life and your ability to stay curious and dream, which is something you should always be able to access and enjoy.

All-or-Nothing/Black-and-White Thinking

All-or-nothing thinking, or black-and-white thinking, forces you to choose one side over another when taking in a feeling or working through a problem. With this type of thinking, something is either *this* over here or *that* over there, without leaving any room for anything in between. This thinking categorizes people, situations, and experiences in extremes, leaving very little room for the gray area between. Your thoughts make judgments that tell you that you are either a winner or a loser, rather than encouraging you to take a chance and try your best.

All-or-nothing thinking reduces your choices and ignores the reality of having more than one feeling at a time. You can feel happy you are graduating from school *and* sad that you will miss your friends, teachers, and coaches at the same time. This type of thinking also limits your ability to connect with others and the colorful, exciting world around you. Mindfulness, however, keeps you in the present and aware of your judgments and decisions, which is a key solution to the all-or-nothing thinking trap.

Labeling

Labeling is when you generalize a one-time experience and assign it an all-the-time label. It is an extreme version of overgeneralization. When you attach your emotions to labeling, it can affect your relationships negatively. Instead of acknowledging that a person made a mistake, you might take a negative path and label that person as a jerk. You can label yourself negatively as well. If you miss a problem on a math quiz, you might be quick to label yourself an idiot, instead of being kind to yourself about the accidental oversight. This extreme form of thinking about things can also cause you to experience extreme feelings and emotions, disappointment and hurt, as if your feelings can only exist on a scale of 1 (super happy) to 10 (super upset), where a score of 5 doesn't even exist! But emotions really do exist on a spectrum, and it's most fair to assess them without extreme labels.

Mindfulness calms these unfair but automatic methods of thinking; it helps you observe judgmental thought patterns and resist thinking in extremes. With mindfulness, you can take a step back and look out on the horizon to see the whole picture instead of just one specific angle. Looking at a situation or feeling objectively and honestly helps you problem solve and build closer relationships. Strictly loving versus hating is a hard way to live life! Feeling happy all the time is neither honest nor realistic, and feeling miserable all the time is unhealthy and can lead one down a dark path into depression. Looking at the spectrum of emotions more honestly, and without judgment, is much more realistic and manageable!

REAL TALK

I met Jane when I was a school social worker at her school when she was in the ninth grade. Her teachers told me she was having a hard time reading, and they were concerned because she didn't participate or talk to anyone. Jane was hard of hearing but had not worn her hearing aids since the fifth grade. When I asked her why she did not wear them, she said, "It's too loud. Everything is loud!" With hearing aids, Jane felt that the world was too loud and chaotic and unlikable. In stark comparison, her world without hearing aids felt calm and comfortable, but it meant feeling isolated.

One morning, I requested that Jane meet me in my office. We made a deal that she would wear her hearing aids, and I would help her with schoolwork. I told her, "I am not a teacher, so please be patient with me. And because you are not used to wearing your hearing aids, be patient with yourself. Hopefully, we will learn that we can do hard things together without judging ourselves." Jane said, "Everyone judges me. I am never going to read out loud well."

When Jane used her hearing aids, she was very annoyed with the hum of the refrigerator in the corner of my office. I pointed out that because I heard it all day, my brain found a way to ignore it. I told Jane, "You can learn this trick, too; it's called incidental noise—my brain tells my ears we don't need to pay attention." As Jane practiced reading aloud, we worked on her learning to tune out any noises of judgment the same way that she tuned out the hum of the refrigerator.

By the end of the year, Jane was confidently reading out loud without judging each word she spoke and without judging herself for reading at all. She made friends, and even joined a sports team. Even though it was difficult at times for her to hear all the noise of the world around her, every day she picked up her hearing aids to use them. She realized that even though she could create a world of calm without them, it also created a world of isolation that cut her off from friends, relationships, sports, and fun—none of which were as chaotic as she initially thought they were. Jane learned that when she let go of the voice of judgment, it became incidental noise. Just like the annoying hum of a refrigerator, she could observe and ignore the sound, and tune in instead to all the other wonderful things around her.

Simple Meditation

1. Go into a room where you feel calm and comfortable without the prying of others (that includes pets!)—this can be your bedroom or someplace outdoors. Sit down in a position that feels comfortable and settle in so you can be open to your thoughts and your body.

2. This may seem strange, but you are going to welcome in judgment. Take a breath and visualize a chair next to you, one where judgment can sit with you. In this moment, judgment isn't in control; it's just allowed to be present.

3. Feel your body and be open to how it feels—fidgety, still, tight, or just there. If you feel yourself drift away, be kind to yourself and bring yourself back.

4. Bring attention to a judgment you made today about yourself. Visualize how it made you feel, which could be in the form of a cloud bubble, a callout, or a text message. If a judgmental thought tells you that you are not enough, allow it to sit next to you and see if it stays.

5. Take a deep breath and tell yourself, "I am enough." Exhale, and breathe in self-love. Tell yourself, "I believe in me."

6. Visualize judgment slouching in the chair. Visualize yourself looking back at the chair and taking a step forward.

7. Take a breath in and out. When you feel your anxiety start judging, remember you are enough.

Judgy Much?

Sometimes you may use judgments to motivate yourself to do better, but it's important to remember that self-love does not look like, or feel like, self-shame or self-loathing. In order for you to release yourself from negative judgment, you need to do some self-research on where it is showing up in your life. For this exercise, you will take a best-friend view of yourself, meaning that you will imagine that you are your own best friend—your number one confidant, the person you can tell your deepest secrets and dreams to, the person who will cheerlead you on and help clear the path to success. Be your best friend and help yourself face some hard truths in the areas in which you judge yourself harshly.

Complete the following sentences:

I judge myself on _____

My negative self-talk shows up when _____

*I feel bad about myself when I judge*_____

*I judge my appearance on*_____

*I judge myself as good or bad on the basis of*_____

Now that you have finished these sentences, be your own best friend and tell yourself not to blame these judgments for existing. Have awareness of these judgments when they show up next time; what is the purpose for them to be here in this moment? Keep yourself accountable by knowing you do not have to categorize yourself. You are more than a checkbox!

Build Gray in a Good Way

In the chart below you'll find some examples of extreme black-and-white thinking. The middle column is blank so you can practice building thoughts and feelings that exist in the gray area between black and white extremes. Go through the chart and explore what comfortable gray thoughts come to mind and write them down. This will help you better recognize when you start to think in extremes and remember that there are feelings in between that will better serve you.

BLACK	BUILD GRAY	WHITE
Good		Bad
Weak		Strong
Obese		Anorexic
Beautiful		Hideous
Stupid		Genius
Calm		Hyper
Sad		Joyous
Structured		Unorganized
Destructive		Creative
Popular		Loner

Reflection: In what areas of your life does black-and-white thinking hinder you from your goals?

Do extreme judgments prevent you from being connected to others in your life? How so? Think of any negative self-talk you might sometimes engage in. What black-and-white thoughts does your brain tell you about yourself where you might benefit from building out some gray area thoughts?

Just Dance!

Music has the power to transform the brain and affect the way it works; it connects your body and brain physically, emotionally, and spiritually. It promotes positive feelings and helps increase self-acceptance. Research has shown that dancing improves creativity and reading skills while also lowering depression and anxiety. Dance and music improve your life through making connections with others and through connecting with your own emotions. Your body has a natural rhythm, such as how you walk and run. Dancing may feel a bit scary sometimes, especially in front of others, but today you are your own audience. Feel free to show yourself your favorite dance moves! It is the perfect thing for you to practice non-judgment with yourself. The goal is to have fun without one drop of shame or negative self-talk.

Turn on your favorite danceable song. If you feel comfortable, you can close your eyes. Listen to the song and let your body dance to the rhythm. Stay focused on how your body moves to the beat. Is the song slower or faster in some sections? How does your body react? Mindfully dance, letting yourself enjoy the music and your sweet dance moves without judgment. If you feel yourself starting to judge, redirect yourself to hear the music and feel your body moving.

YOU'VE GOT THIS!

"I have yet to reach my full potential. I am unique, and my talents grow each day. I commit to myself to build awareness of my judgments. I will mindfully believe in myself. I will dedicate time to observe myself as I work toward being the best version of me, one day at a time from today forward."

I See You

Overthinking and judgment are close cousins. Anxiety can cause you to overthink, question, and judge yourself or others. For this mindful exercise, you are going to use your imagination and a visualization technique to look thoughtfully at yourself. Visualization helps improve the ability to cope in stressful periods and relax; it adds to your physical and mental fitness and overall wellness. The goal for this visualization is to build self-compassion where you can observe your thoughts toward yourself without hiding them or ignoring them. If you'd like, you can do this exercise with calm, instrumental music playing in the background to help eliminate any distracting noise.

1. Close your eyes and picture another physical version of you facing yourself.

2. Think of all the feelings you feel toward yourself: love, bitterness, pride, annoyance, friendship, shame, insecurity, etc. You may also feel completely neutral today.

3. Looking at yourself across from you, see the struggles and challenges that you are dealing with or have overcome. Without judgment for those struggles, be present in your feelings in this moment. You are seeing yourself this way for the first time in this moment—perfectly imperfect.

4. Now visualize the sun shining on you, projecting warmth and light. Feel the feelings you want to send to yourself: love, forgiveness, understanding, affection, joy, or calmness.

5. Tune in to your body feeling lighter, feeling warmer, almost like you can feel yourself across from you giving you a hug.

You can do this exercise for several minutes. It is a great way to honor yourself and all that you are. You may want to start your day with this exercise and use it as an intention to stay present and have compassion for yourself throughout the day.

Hit Pause!

Time is a wizard—some days can feel slow while other days fly right on by. Today you are going to hit the Pause button and be your own wizard. Pausing will give you the opportunity to take a moment to recharge and check in, especially if you are feeling overwhelmed or if the sound of judgment is too loud. You check in to see how your friends are doing, but how often do you check in on yourself? Checking in on your feelings and where you are at in this moment and throughout the day can help manage your anxiety. This kind of reflection helps you better access the small voice that guides you to think positively. When you pause, you feel that much more cared for and connected.

Here are some ways you can mindfully pause:

Breathe: Breathing helps you come back to your body and makes space for you to check in on your feelings. Stay conscious and breathe purposefully in and out. Take a few deep breaths as you pause in this moment.

Draw, doodle, color: Being creative for even a few minutes can help you feel present in the moment and establish a sense of calm. Creativity allows your imagination to blossom and lets positive energy lead the way.

Be in nature: Being outside for a few minutes and noticing the beauty of the sky, a flower, or a singing bird can connect you to the world around you and remind you of the beauty and value of what you may take for granted.

What pause do you need today?

Judgy[2]

Often your own inner critic shapes what you do and how you feel. With the *Judgy Much?* exercise on page 41, you were your own best friend and helped bring awareness to the areas in which you judge yourself. In this exercise, you'll take a third-person approach to build awareness on when anxiety shows up. Think of it as if you are standing outside your body, observing and guiding your thoughts. Allow this third person to guide you to safely feel your feelings of anxiety and tell you what you need to hear so that judgments are not the loudest voice.

Guide: Your anxiety shows up when you judge yourself on . . .

Guide: It seems like when your anxiety shows up you need . . .

Guide: You feel anxious when you hear yourself use negative self-talk. You know you feel anxious when you tell yourself . . .

Guide: It seems like it would be helpful to tell yourself an affirmation, like . . .

Guide: You feel anxiety about yourself when you hear others judge you on . . .

Guide: To let go of the judgment, tell yourself that you are . . .

Guide: If you judge your friends, it can feel like judging yourself. Your anxiety becomes a lot to manage when . . .

Guide: Your friends are amazing and care about you. What is one thing you are grateful for that they add to your friendship?

Guide: You sometimes judge your family for . . .

Guide: If you could tell your family about your anxiety, what would be important for them to know so they could help?

MINDFUL MOMENT

Each day, you can practice living nonjudgmentally in the moment. Recall the story about Jane, who was hesitant to wear her hearing aids because the noise of the world was so loud and extreme. It was when Jane gave herself permission to hear the world and engage with it that she realized what she was missing out on. Our nonjudgmental on/off switch has a dimmer where you can build the more comfortable and realistic hues of gray. Building gray will help you foster the voice that guides you to healthy relationships, healthy thoughts, and more resources to manage your anxiety. Give yourself permission to hear your small voice and be open to the world and people around you without worry. Sign the permission slip below to commit to living nonjudgmentally from today forward as best as you can.

PERMISSION SLIP

I agree to the following commitments:

→ I give myself permission to observe my judgments.
→ I will not judge my judgments.
→ I will practice developing hues of gray.
→ I will pause when I feel myself being judgmental.
→ I will visualize myself being the best version of myself.
→ I will listen to the inner voice that cheers me on when things are difficult.

Sign Here: _____

POSITIVE VIBES

"Today I let go of judgment and welcome ingenuity! When life gives me LIMES instead of lemons, I can switch things up and turn them into a SMILE. I can take my SMILE and travel MILES each day!"

YOUR TAKEAWAYS

"A day spent judging another is a painful day. A day spent judging yourself is a painful day."

— Buddha

→ You learned that judgment could cloud your experiences and relationships, thereby filtering your life through likes and dislikes.

→ Anxiety patterns can make you think in limiting ways that are only black and white. These patterns skew your thinking and cause extremes of emotion, disappointment, and hurt. Living and developing hues of gray will help you maintain a healthy balance.

→ Building self-compassion is a practice just like mindfulness, and you can do it with intention each day through visualization.

→ Letting go of judgment frees you from living and thinking in a box. When you remove unhelpful filters such as these, you're able to see life for what it really is and build stronger connections.

→ Giving yourself permission to change your thinking habits will help you feel calm and content.

Idea Questions

→ How will you practice non-judgment toward yourself? Toward others?

→ What do you need to tell yourself when you feel tempted to use the labeling machine to categorize your life?

→ How will releasing yourself from judgment leave you feeling lighter and happier?

→ Which exercise will you use to confidently walk the path of living nonjudgmentally?

CHAPTER FOUR

IT IS WHAT IT IS

As Jon Kabat-Zinn said, "You cannot stop the waves, but you can learn to surf." The waves of life will always roll, but you can learn to surf those waves with mindfulness! Throughout this chapter you will build your own surfboard for the waves of life, one exercise at a time, adding other special mindfulness accessories—like a safety leash or your network of friends, family, and trusted adults who you can lean on throughout the process—for even more support. Stay reflective and open as you learn to surf: *it is what it is.* There are days where the storm is rough with anxiety and emotion. Acceptance is a process of learning and growing. You will learn to surf through developing the mindfulness principle of acceptance, helping you create peace one wave at a time.

THE MINDFUL WAY

Every morning when you open your eyes, you set sail for the day. Some days the weather is stormy and the water is rough; other days the water is flat and you can see far and wide. Most days there is at least a ripple that rocks your boat. In order to navigate the waters safely and successfully, you develop safety nets and lifeboats through the people you trust and love. There are some circumstances you can control; as an example, you woke up today and chose to read this book. But there are many moments when you have to accept that "it is what it is," like the waves crashing against the boat and having to balance the storm. Those waves may be relatively small but are still stressful. Examples of small waves in your day may be procrastinating instead of doing your homework, spacing on texting someone back, or forgetting to charge your cell phone. In these moments, you can feel annoyance, anxiety, frustration, anger, or sadness. *It is what it is,* though, and you can accept that; you simply forgot to do the homework, you forgot to communicate with someone, or your cell battery is on low for the day—and everything will still be okay. This is the process for developing self-compassion, when you accept yourself and are kind to yourself the way you would be to a friend.

Acceptance is the act of your mind embracing experiences, feelings, thoughts, and situations without reacting defensively with avoidance or denial. The secret to acceptance is to know it is an active psychological process. When uncomfortable moments happen, you may have your defenses ready. To build psychological acceptance and turn it into a mindfulness practice, you might have to tell these defenses that it is okay to be uncomfortable in these moments. You can remind yourself that you have support systems ready, and do not have to spend all of your energy fighting. Acceptance can be very powerful and allows you to stop zooming in on what is wrong or not going right in the moment. It allows you to focus on other things like what you are feeling, which senses you are using in the moment, and what is happening around you that you are able to notice. Being present will help you take that essential step forward.

When you feel stressed, it diminishes your experiences. Your focus is shifted away from the moment, causing you to miss out. You cannot enjoy your experiences because your mind and body are so focused on the feeling of stress. Acceptance, however, allows things to run their natural course, which allows your mind and body to relax and produce lower levels of cortisol, the stress hormone your body makes when you feel fear or stress.

Through acceptance, you are able to look in the mirror and embrace yourself exactly as you are without feeling compelled to force yourself to be something you are not. When you try to force yourself to do or feel something, often through denial or avoidance, it is hard to know how to move forward, because you are not seeing a situation for what it is. In order to move forward in a healthy way, the first step is to lower your defenses and open yourself to standing in the light and being seen. Get out there and show yourself! Even though you may feel uncomfortable, even if your anxiety is with you, stay brave. When you do this, your mind is less likely to wander off and will be less reactive to stress. Accepting yourself in the moment, such as right now as you read these words one at a time, allows you to apply your inner wisdom to a situation. Rather than feeling overwhelmed by stress or avoiding people or situations, you can lean into the moment, be more transparent, and better communicate your needs. Acceptance teaches you to name your thoughts and feelings and lean into a calmer state. It helps you roll out a welcome mat for your feelings, telling yourself, "It is okay to not be okay."

COMMON ANXIETY PATTERNS

Anxiety can make you feel small, unworthy, or undeserving. As a result, your thought patterns can fall into two cognitive distortions where you mentally filter out the positive and focus on the negative, or else you minimize yourself and discount your abilities. Let's dig into this a bit more to better understand these common anxiety patterns—where they come from, what they mean, and how to combat them.

Mental Filtering

In addition to the ways in which your perspective can filter how you see things, mental filtering happens when you filter out the positives and concentrate on one detail that is negative. Imagine that you took an exam, and out of a hundred questions, you only got two wrong, and earned an "A" grade. Ideally, you'd be so proud of the fact that you earned an "A," but if all you can focus on is the fact that you got two questions wrong and you tell yourself that you did not study enough, or that you are not smart, you're mentally filtering the positive to focus on the negative. It's also possible that you could be so proud of your good grade that you mentally filter the positive in a way that sets an unrealistic level of expectations, such as performing perfectly on every exam. If you were to mentally filter that impossible goal, it might set you up for failure and increase your sense of anxiety and stress. Dwelling on either extreme through mental filtering isn't rooted in reality, and in fact, it skews your vision of yourself, which can cause low self-esteem or have other negative effects.

Minimizing

Another form of cognitive distortion would be to receive an "A" on your exam but quickly minimize your achievements, even to the point that you make yourself feel undeserving, or like an impostor. Regardless of your accomplishments, you can easily make yourself feel like an impostor if you filter your feelings and ideas through anxiety, rather than through mindfulness. It is quite natural to do so, but try your best to cut yourself some slack. Even Einstein had self-doubt about his accomplishments, and many considered him the most famous scientist in the world. Impostorism, also known as "impostor syndrome," can be felt by all people, across all ages and races, but remember that while it may be a psychological phenomenon, it isn't a disease. Psychologist and professor Dr. Pauline Rose Clance was the first to observe impostorism among college students when they talked about their feelings of self-doubt. Some truly believed that they were not as smart as their colleagues, despite being in the same school, taking the same classes, and earning good grades. Dr. Clance consulted with psychologist Dr. Suzanne Imes, and together they created the term "impostor phenomenon," which succinctly accounted for the ways in which people can filter their feelings and accomplishments in such a way that minimizes them to unhealthy and unfair extremes.

When your brain uses these two distortions, filtering and minimizing, it changes your reality, and you begin to feel like you do not deserve all you have and are not as awesome as others might really think. The distortions discount your achievements, successes, and talents and convince you that you must just get lucky sometimes, even when you're very talented and working really hard. Shaking off these feelings can be difficult if they take a strong root in your mind, but they can be even harder to shake off if you don't say them out loud or lean on someone for support in the moment that you are feeling them. Mindfulness is a great and effective way to quiet the thought patterns because it helps you see and accept yourself exactly as you are—perfectly imperfect.

REAL TALK

Michael came into my office, sat down without saying hello, and asked, "How did you pick the colleges you applied to?" I looked down and started laughing. I said, "I put all my eggs in one basket and only applied to one school. But I do not recommend that strategy." Michael looked confused. "Are you lying? That's a joke, right?" When I asked Michael what schools he was applying to, he dispassionately named a handful of schools, as though he was ordering off a menu, and it struck me that he didn't mention a school I knew he really wanted to attend. As soon as I asked about the school I hadn't heard him mention, he snorted in response. "Miss, there is no way I am getting in there." I thought that this response was really strange; Michael is in the top of his class! "Michael, why do you think that?" He looked at me and said, "I am not the right type of student."

I reassured Michael that everyone has their own unique path to college, but that most share a similar finish line—a diploma, a college degree, and pride. Michael shook his head. "I don't think I can do it. I feel like I am in my own way." I asked Michael what classes he was taking, and he listed five Advanced Placement classes, the hardest classes his school had to offer. Then, it was like a spark went off in his brain. "If I pass all these AP tests, I will be a semester ahead." I said, "It seems to me that if you are taking the hardest classes, you must be a smart and capable student. Your counselor wouldn't let you take all those classes if you couldn't handle it." Michael smiled and said, "You think I can get into the college I really want to go to?" I smiled back and replied, "Not if you don't apply!" He stood up, turned around, and declared, "Not only will I apply, but I'll be a semester ahead!"

It was a real mic-drop moment when Michael realized he was enough. Sure, there might be moments when anxiety tells you that you're not adequate, when you mentally filter and minimize your positive attributes and accomplishments, or when fear causes you to focus on the obstacles instead of the reward, but talking it through with someone you trust can help bring you back to the present moment, put those negative filters down, and believe in yourself in the same way that those around you believe in you, too.

Eyes Open

For this simple meditation, think of your mood and the moods of others as a weather forecast—sun for good days and positive thoughts, and rain and clouds for tougher days and negative thoughts. Acceptance will help you fully live without judgment and help embrace an open, curious mind.

1. Find a calm and quiet place to sit where you will feel safe and free to think.

2. Take a deep breath and clear your mind of judgment, worry, and to-dos. This is an opportunity for less stress and a place to mentally embrace yourself.

3. Imagine moods and ideas as weather and how, like the weather, you cannot control others; your sunshine is not dependent on their actions, and vice versa. Close your eyes and visualize your personal weather forecast. What does it look like at this hour?

4. Breathe in as you identify your feelings. If you can hear any noise, welcome it and stay curious as to the source. Any thoughts or feelings that may come to mind are your teachers in building acceptance.

5. Take a deep breath and notice how you feel: Let your chest and stomach move as they do without feeling like you need to control them. Feel your body from the inside to the outside. Know that you do not need to be anyone else but you in this moment, and your journey on this path is right where you need to be. Take in any feeling with acceptance.

6. Take a deep breath and say to yourself, "I am enough, I believe in myself, I accept all that is good and all the challenges in my life. I am who I choose to be in this moment."

7. Take another breath, in and out, massage your eyes in a circular motion, and open them when you feel comfortable. Engage your world as *it is what it is.*

Where Are You?

The path of acceptance is all about being connected to the present moment, where you can feel your feelings and be aware of your emotions. To explore your level of awareness and build acceptance, respond to the 10 statements below with a mark, such as your favorite symbol, a star, an X, or a check. Focus on one statement at a time. If you drift off as you're reading through the statements, gently bring your attention back, and answer as honestly as you can with a nonjudgmental and beginner's mind. There are no right answers; it is what it is.

MINDFUL STATEMENT	ALWAYS	OFTEN	SOMETIMES	RARELY	NEVER
I am aware of my emotions.					
I try not to think about my problems.					
I am able to recognize and communicate my feelings to others.					
I avoid thinking about parts of myself that I feel bad about.					
I can feel my anxiety in my body.					
I can feel my emotions changing with awareness.					
I redirect my thoughts when a negative memory comes to mind.					
I am aware of the facial expressions I make when speaking to others.					

MINDFUL STATEMENT	ALWAYS	OFTEN	SOMETIMES	RARELY	NEVER
I try not to think of things that make me feel sad.					
I am in touch with my senses, such as how my body feels, the feel of the chair, what I see around me, when I sit down, etc.					

Reflect: Mindfulness helps build attention to where you are and establishes a desire for learning, being open, being curious, and practicing acceptance. If you responded "Never" to most of the statements, you can use mindfulness and acceptance to eventually respond "Always" to these statements. Remember, acceptance is a process.

DJ Me

Music is a great way to focus yourself in the moment, feel connected to the world around you, and stay mindful throughout the day. If you are a musician, this can also help you be more attentive as you play! Make a playlist of five new songs to help you redirect yourself to the present moment; they can belong to any genre and can contain lyrics or be instrumental only. If you're unsure of where to start, add one of your favorite songs so you know you'll get lost in singing along and enjoying the moment. When you listen to the other four songs, stay present through each word and every note. The goal for this exercise is to listen and be in tune with your body and mind, accepting where you are in this moment.

DJ Set List

1. _____

2. _____

3. _____

4. _____

5. _____

Think about times when music can help you lower your stress and anxiety. Is it in the morning when you need to get inspired to tackle a big to-do list? In the evening when you need to calm a racing mind? While you're doing homework and need to focus? Reflect on your typical day and decide where each song might fit in; you're the DJ!

DJ Set List Plan

1. _____

2. _____

3. _____

4. _____

5. _____

Get in There, Coach

The act of filtering and minimizing prevents you from being present. Those cognitive distortions ignore the positives of a situation or feeling and focus instead on what you think is missing. Feelings of inadequacy prevent you from moving forward and challenging yourself to achieve the rewards that await you. When this happens, you need to remove the impostor in your life and replace them with an inspiring and encouraging coach. As the late, great Kobe Bryant said, "The beauty of coaching is growing the players from the ground up. That journey continues." Invest in yourself on this journey and shake off any feelings of doubt. You deserve someone in your corner to remind you how far you've come and where you're heading!

In the chart below, write down minimizing phrases or thoughts that you have sometimes in the left column, and then write down how you will champion yourself in the right column. If you encounter the impostor mindset while doing this, be sure to introduce it to your number one coach—you!

MINIMIZING THOUGHT	COACHING ADVICE
I am not a great artist.	You are an incredible artist! People tell you how much they love your art daily.

MINIMIZING THOUGHT	COACHING ADVICE

Reflect: If you feel comfortable, tell someone you trust about a minimizing thought you often have. Feedback is a great way to bolster how you coach yourself and to find coaches in others.

YOU'VE GOT THIS!

Life gives you obstacles and hurdles not to hurt you but to help you grow. Each day that you encounter any obstacles or hurdles, find a way to accept them for what they are as you find your way around them—whether it's jumping over, crawling under, or digging a tunnel toward the solution on the other side. Today, try to see these obstacles for what they are: an opportunity to practice acceptance, flex your problem-solving skills, and learn a life lesson.

Two Taps to Less Stress

Emotional Freedom Tapping (EFT) is the act of therapeutically tapping on specific points of the body to relieve physical and emotional pain, restore a feeling of balance, and produce oxytocin in the brain, which helps you feel trusting and empathetic. (Trust and empathy also help you accept and love yourself without judgment.) Tapping is an easy and a convenient way to help regulate your emotions when you feel stress or become overwhelmed. In this exercise, each tap uses two fingers—your index and middle finger—to make two taps, one and two; think of it like pushing a button with two fingers. You can practice on a surface first if you'd like. You may want to read the directions out loud to yourself and then follow along after doing so.

Repeat the following mantra as you tap: *"I accept myself. I accept all that I am and all that I am not. I accept my perfectly imperfect self."*

1. With your index and middle fingers together, tap your inner wrists two times switching your left and right wrist, for two rounds. Each side should have four taps total.
2. Tap your shoulders using the same side hand (right hand and right shoulder) at the top of your arms two times on each side.
3. Continue tapping your shoulders, moving your tapping fingers toward your collarbone making a tapping a horizontal line across your chest. Keeping tapping on the horizontal line back to the edge of your shoulders and arms.
4. Now, move your hands to your face; make tapping circles around your eyes.
5. Tap your temples, into your jaw, down the line of your chin.

6. Reverse back the way you started. Chin, jaw, temples, eyes. Then, tap the center of your chest on your collarbone line out to your shoulders. End on your wrists.
7. Take a deep breath and notice how your body feels.

What was the most calming and centering place to tap on your body? When you begin to feel anxiety, or when you notice the first sign of stress, accept the feeling for what it is and use the tapping method in your preferred spot, while breathing in and out.

Kindness/Gratitude Challenge

It can be easier to give kindness to others than it is to give kindness to yourself. Instead of extending compassion and care to yourself, you might fall into the traps of judgment, comparison, perfectionism, and unrealistic expectations. The path to acceptance is all about being kind to yourself. Practicing positive self-talk and gratitude—which research confirms helps you feel less stress and more optimistic about life overall—are two great ways to help your kindness flow more easily, especially when you do it on a regular basis.

Each day this week, challenge yourself to write down one thing you'd like to compliment yourself on, or show yourself gratitude for. Use a mason jar or zip-top bag to collect your compliments and at the end of the week, reflect on the compliments or moments of gratitude.

Some examples of compliments that you could offer yourself include these:

→ *Way to stay kind when others were not.*

→ *High five on studying and managing your anxiety during the test.*

→ *Good job on that presentation in class, you nailed it!*

→ *It was great to see you challenge yourself today.*

Some examples of gratitude that you could show yourself include these:

→ *Thank you for taking care of yourself and brushing your teeth.*

→ *I am really grateful you have such caring friends.*

→ *Thank you for saying no when I was feeling overwhelmed.*

→ *I'm grateful you turned off your phone when I needed a quiet break.*

Hey You

Write a small love note to yourself, reflecting on all of the hard and amazing work you've done so far to manage your anxiety and practice mindfulness. You can use the following statements as a guide:

→ *I will be my own coach this week in order to help myself focus on . . .*

→ *I will cheer myself on when I feel uncomfortable because . . .*

→ *I need to be kind to myself in the following ways . . .*

→ *I will practice acceptance and self-compassion by . . .*

MINDFUL MOMENT

Everyone experiences waves of stress or discomfort that come and go. Throughout this chapter, you learned how accepting these waves makes it easier to steer your ship forward and that the secret to accepting oneself is to remember that it is an act, one that you get better at the more you do it. When the waves hit you hard with anxiety, you can safely navigate those waves by embracing them for what they are through acceptance. Be as kind to yourself as you are to others and practice self-compassion as you ride each wave. When you feel yourself filtering out the positive, call on your trusty inner coach to get back on track and feel good. You can use gratitude each day to develop awareness of all that you have to offer the world. Take a deep breath and tell yourself you are enough in this moment right now. Onward!

POSITIVE VIBES

The voice in your head that tells you that you're not enough can be a whisper some days and an amplified scream on other days. Author Brené Brown advises you to "let go of who you think you are supposed to be and be who you are."

Affirmation: *"I am who I am supposed to be, perfectly imperfectly me. I accept all my talents and all my flaws; they make me uniquely me."*

YOUR TAKEAWAYS

"If you do something with acceptance and kindness, you can create a true friendship."

— Dustin Lance Black

→ In order for you to have psychological acceptance and accept yourself, you have to lower your defenses to let in the good. You can remind yourself of the support in your life to achieve this comfortably.

→ When you let go of the idea of what or who you should be, that is when you will begin to accept your perfectly imperfect self.

→ Mental filtering and minimizing focus on your deficits, which discounts all the wonderful, positive things about you and your life. Focus on the good!

→ Therapeutic self-touch, such as tapping, can relieve stress and increase self-compassion.

Idea Questions

→ How will you practice acceptance this week?

→ When you feel yourself mentally filtering, what will be your affirmation to stand tall?

→ How will you show yourself compassion this week?

→ What is the most inspiring takeaway from this chapter?

CHAPTER FIVE

ONE STEP AT A TIME

It is estimated that across the world there are more than 70,000 internet searches per second, 3.8 million per minute, 5.8 billion per day, and 2 trillion a year! Technology has created instant gratification, which means that patience is not as common as perhaps it used to be. When you want to find something out, you can look it up instantly—no flipping through dense encyclopedias at the library to find the answer. When you want to purchase something, you search, click, and buy, and it ships to your door almost instantly. All the truly essential things in life, however, such as your relationships, friendships, family, accomplishments, and passions, still take patience to find, nurture, and maintain. Sometimes you even need to overcome challenges in order to reach your goals—there's no next-day shipping for success. Patience helps you build resilience, the ability to bounce back and adapt, when you face challenges and roadblocks. One step at a time, you can learn to practice patience, slowing your anxiety down for you to stay present. Don't think of it as delaying gratification, but rather appreciating the process to successfully live in each and every special moment.

THE MINDFUL WAY

Patience is the ability to endure difficulty and maintain calm and control. It is through patience that you can suppress restlessness, annoyance, frustration, anger, and instead persevere, stay composed, and be present in the moment. To have patience is a virtue, but it's also a reflection of your values; relationships take time and investment on an individual level and on a collective level. Think of your closest friend—they were not your best friend the first moment you met them. But you saw potential and decided that the friendship was a worthwhile investment, and you practiced patience to allow the relationship to grow from casual friendship to best friendship.

It isn't always easy, or second nature, to practice patience, and sometimes you can even be impatient with yourself. When this happens, your brain becomes frustrated and begins to doubt itself, which in turn lets shame and anxiety creep in. When you're feeling internally impatient, you may hear your self-talk asking you unfair questions like "Why aren't you good at this?" or offering up negative statements like "You're so slow. You are going to be behind." Impatience can make you feel like you need to rush ahead to the next feeling or experience, which robs you of feeling the joy of the present moment. When this happens, it's hard to be mindful; you are a few steps ahead mentally, and your body is two steps behind.

Taking things one step at a time helps you be patient with yourself and with others. When you are able to slow down and hold your ground, you not only feel calmer but also make fewer mistakes. Living life in fast-forward mode may mean that you get a lot of things done, but the cost is that you never truly enjoy the ride. Being patient with yourself allows you to develop empathy and self-compassion, which ultimately helps you be patient with others and supports your relationships to be that much healthier, more positive, and less stressful.

In order to practice patience, you need to first understand what triggers you to feel impatient. I know sometimes I move so fast, like the Energizer Bunny—going, going, gone—and I discovered that my trigger is when I feel overwhelmed, have a full to-do list, or see a jam-packed schedule. The people who care about me have helped me build awareness when I am blinded by the next thing. I realize I have overcommitted and missed setting a boundary for myself.

Think of your triggers. What sets off your anxiety alarm bell? Is it being overscheduled with homework and projects? One trigger that may impact you is when you set a goal for yourself; often you may seek the end result without being present throughout the process. The process of reaching that goal has a path of growth and learning. How does your body react in these moments when you are focused on what is next? Remind yourself that things take time, especially important things. How do the people who care about you help you build awareness? They may model patience to you or make suggestions on slowing down to enjoy the moment. You might also need to ask for support in order to build awareness to slow down.

When you are able to slow down, you have wisdom in decision-making. You are able to see that things come in their own time, such as building friendships, getting good at something, school, etc. Patience helps you accept your path that is unique to you. It provides comfort in the fact that the time it takes to get somewhere is a worthwhile journey and you can focus on the present moment each step along the way. Developing the attitude of patience will help you bounce back and adapt when these twists and turns come about. The twists and turns and barriers and hurdles often teach you problem-solving, and you evolve your decision-making skills. They force you to slow down because you have to seek a solution or an answer. Patience will release you from the demands of life and allow you to welcome challenges as opportunities.

COMMON ANXIETY PATTERNS

Your thoughts can feel like a relay race that you never signed up for. One thought leads to another and before you know it, you've jumped to a conclusion that isn't evidence based, rewrote the narrative of what happened, or predicted the future, all from a place of fear. When you do this, you often wind up feeling defeated, and leave little room for there to be a different, and more satisfactory, next chapter or ending to your story. Anxious, racing thoughts make change feel impossible and make you think that success is a distant, unattainable target. Rest assured, however, that that is not really the case! By identifying these different anxiety patterns, you can stop them in their tracks, and be well on your way to a patient and mindful mindset.

Mind Reading

When you attempt to mind read—which isn't the fun form of mysticism, but rather an example of anxious thought patterns—you assume that people are thinking negative thoughts about you and reacting poorly to you without any evidence that this is actually true. Mind reading can cloud your mind so intensely that you wind up making innocent but anxious mistakes when it comes to social cues and norms because you operate from the negative reality that you created in your mind rather than the reality that you're actually operating in. Doing so can negatively impact your mood and cause anxiety in social situations, and even in your relationships with people who you know love and care about you. You may smile at your coach, and they may continue walking without any obvious facial expression. You mind read that they are mad at you and were disappointed at your performance. In reality, your coach was thinking of the game schedule and how they needed to change the practice times. Now, you may feel awkward or hyperaware of your coach's responses to you. However, mind reading can be helpful in moments when someone you meet smiles at you and you smile back, offering positivity in exchange. It is important to be cautious and be aware when mind reading fosters negativity and fear.

Fortune-Telling

No, sadly this isn't the cool kind of fortune-telling that you're thinking of. Fortune-telling in relation to anxious thoughts is when you struggle to take things in as they are because anxiety is clouding your mind, and instead you try to predict a negative outcome. You might tell yourself that things are going to end badly, you will fail, and that you should be afraid because something awful is going to happen. Think about times that you are running late for something, even just by two minutes. Do you automatically think you are going to get in trouble? That everyone will be mad at you? That you will fail the test because you will not have enough time to finish? Sure, sometimes there are consequences for being really late to obligations, but in reality, most times two minutes is not going to be a life-altering amount of time. If you're late to class, at worst your teacher may be mildly annoyed, and at best they'll be understanding. Having two minutes less time on a test does not mean you will fail the entire test. Anxiety sometimes pressures you to fortune-tell out of fear, but not because it's the actual truth.

Catastrophizing

Your ordinary worries can turn into ugly monsters when you think that the absolute worst thing ever will happen. If worry and anxiety are out of control in that way, you begin to dread normal everyday things and situations and turn them into a catastrophe. Think of a class that you find challenging—when your anxiety is at an all-time high, do you tell yourself that you will *never* do well in the class, even if the truth is that, with the help of a tutor or a little extra studying, you will be just fine? You might compound the situation at hand by using your anxious fortune-telling skills and imagining a situation turning into a full-blown catastrophe. When you catastrophize, you try to anticipate every little thing that might, under the "right" circumstances, go wrong and immediately assume that you should expect the worst possible outcome. The truth is that you can't predict the future, and it doesn't serve you to envision a failing grade on an exam before you even read the first question.

It is important to be aware of when your brain is drawing its own conclusions and attempting to predict the future—that awareness will allow you to slow down your anxious thoughts before they run wild. In that moment, take a deep breath, acknowledge that anxiety is impacting your ability to be patient, and stay within the moment and the process. Practicing patience also allows you to show yourself compassion. One moment does not define you, and developing the attitude of patience will release the pressure of what is yet to come.

REAL TALK

Trey volunteered in my office and was always willing to help. One morning, I saw Trey throw his backpack off and sit down. His face looked flat—no emotion, no smile, no sadness—and he was completely silent. "Good morning Trey, what is going on?" I asked. Trey said, "There is so much pressure, I don't even have fun anymore. It's do this, do that, be this thing . . . If you want to be successful, you have to satisfy the demands of the future now." I walked over, sat next to Trey, and said, "It sounds like you are having a rough day. Expectations— homework, school, sports, family—can weigh on you each day; think of them as tiny marbles filling up a jar. Some days, it can feel like they are multiplying and piling up and putting pressure on you to take care of them very quickly, especially when your jar fills up quicker than you anticipate."

Trey began to realize the feeling that his jar was overflowing with marbles of obligations and expectations, and that it did not happen overnight. Slowly one marble became two, and two marbles became six, and so on. He said, "I feel so anxious, like I'm spiraling, like I'm not even in control." I reassured Trey that was a very normal way to feel and reminded him that he could use patience and mindfulness to feel more in control and begin to empty out the jar of marbles. Trey said, "I can visualize myself here, in this moment, slow my thoughts down, and stay present." Trey told me he did this in a baseball game when he was up to bat and it really helped. We agreed that just like baseball, mindfulness is a skill; practicing being patient and waiting for the ball to come your way when you're up at bat is a skill. And when your skills grow stronger, that helps them become habits, and that helps you play your best and even win the game.

After talking it through, Trey was able to accept himself and acknowledge the marbles in his jar that represented anxious thoughts and pressures. Practicing the attitude of patience can help you pay attention to one marble at a time—the one that needs to be dealt with, can be dealt with, and should be dealt with. With this approach, your jar of marbles won't reach the top and overflow; practicing patience helps you balance things in the present moment by acknowledging the anxious feeling, slowing down, and taking in only what it needs.

Just Be

When life feels fast paced, it can feel challenging to be patient with yourself. "How can I really be patient when I exist in a world ruled by instant gratification?" It is possible, though, and it is incredibly helpful to practice patience in the face of anxious thoughts and feelings. The following meditation will give you permission to *just be* with the process.

1. Lie down in a place where you feel safe and will be uninterrupted for at least five minutes.

2. Breathe in for four counts—1, 2, 3, 4—and out for four counts—1, 2, 3, 4. Count backward from 10 and continue to breathe in a natural rhythm. Pay attention to how you feel in this moment. If you need to breathe on the count of 4 again, do so.

3. Feel yourself deepening into a relaxed state. Close your eyes if you feel comfortable. Give yourself permission to learn patience in this moment.

4. Visualize a blue sky with wispy clouds slowly drifting from left to right. Feel yourself watching them without thinking where they are going; simply see them and be with them as they drift in the sky. Breathe in and out and watch patiently.

5. Visualize that the cottony clouds have been pulled into thin wisps. Feel yourself feeling lighter, as if you, too, are drifting slowly and patiently by like the clouds. If your thoughts feel like they need to do something, tell yourself this is exactly what you are supposed to be doing—being patient and present in this moment.

6. Take a deep breath in and out. Let yourself sit up and stand up when you are ready. Say to yourself, "I can be patient with myself and others today."

Take What YOU Need

It's important to be aware of your needs and stay present with yourself. One great way to do this is to use an affirmation, like the ones listed below, and either copy them into the Notes app on your phone or write them on a Post-it Note and carry them in your wallet/purse. This way you can carry your affirmation with you, and when you want to cultivate the mindful intention, it will be right there with you, helping you take what you need when you need it.

→ In this moment I choose to be kind; I choose to be patient with myself and others.

→ Time will always continue, and I need to stay present in this moment today.

→ I breathe in patience and breathe out frustration and impatience.

→ I will focus on the task at hand today and not worry about what is next.

→ In this moment I have everything; I am right where I need to be.

→ On this voyage, I will stand with the waves, taking in what I can learn and observe.

→ I have 24 hours a day to be my best self. Each moment, I will receive the opportunities that come my way.

→ When I rush things, something is usually left behind. Everything will stay together as I stay patient.

→ Today, I will listen patiently to myself and others; I will be respectful and respond with kindness.

→ When I feel myself hurrying, I will remember that I set the pace.

Right Hand, Left Hand–Left Hand, Right Hand

Although you may not think of yourself as a teacher, life did in fact hire you! In this exercise you will act as your own teacher and student and practice being patient with yourself as you try to learn something new. Today, you will challenge yourself by copying down the following affirmation with your nondominant hand (90 percent of people are right-handed—if you are left-handed, way to stand out!). Set a timer for 45 seconds and see how many words of the affirmation you can get through. If you feel frustrated, take a deep breath and remind yourself to show yourself patience. Know that you can become ambidextrous with practice and patience!

I can learn anything when I believe in and challenge myself. I need to stay kind to myself as I embark on this voyage. I will approach each wave with patience no matter how easy or hard it feels.

Reflect:

→ Was there a moment you needed to be kind to yourself?

_____

_____

→ How did you practice patience while doing this exercise?

_____

_____

Mini-tation

In moments where your anxiety heightens, you need to recalibrate and shift the attention back to a place of calm. But what if you don't have the time or space for a full-scale meditation? You can do a mini-meditation, which will give you a way to practice patience and establish a sense of calm and self-reflection so you can continue to make good choices and build positive relationships.

Balloon

→ Picture an uninflated balloon in your favorite color.

→ Visualize the balloon being filled with air.

→ Take a deep breath counting backward from 5—5, 4, 3, 2, 1.

→ Breathe in again and exhale like you are blowing up the balloon—5, 4, 3, 2, 1.

→ Repeat until the balloon feels full and you feel relaxed.

Stretch

→ Take a deep breath and raise both hands in the air above your head like you are reaching up to the ceiling.

→ Take a deep breath in and a deep breath out.

→ Wiggle your fingers and bring them down and around to your back.

→ Fold your hands together and push your shoulder blades to the back.

→ Lift your chin up to the ceiling and take a deep breath in and out.

At the end of either mini-meditation, tell yourself, *I can be patient in this moment right now, right here.*

It took Tesla three years to make an electric vehicle prototype before Elon Musk became the company's CEO. Musk said, "Patience is a virtue, and I'm learning patience. It's a tough lesson." Now, Tesla is ranked 124 on the Fortune 500 list, proof that patience pays off!

Affirmation: *"The climb to space is just as important as the arrival. Stay present and enjoy the ride up and down. Each moment is an opportunity for a new view."*

White Space

High expectations paired with busy schedules can leave you feeling overwhelmed—so many competing priorities want you to show up for them and give them all of your energy and attention. Often, you're not even aware of how overscheduled or stressed you feel because you are moving too fast to be mindful of your feelings. The most important question to ask is, when are you showing up for you? One effective solution is to find free time in your calendar and schedule some uninterrupted "me time," which can be whatever you need it to be: reading this book, meditating, listening to music, exercising, etc.

For this exercise, you will intentionally not be using an electronic calendar, but rather the written calendar below. This is because using electronic calendars can be reactionary versus thoughtful. Additionally, research shows that there are positive cognitive effects that result from physically writing with pen and paper. Looking at the week's schedule below, block out 20 minutes each day to refuel yourself with the activity of your choice.

SUNDAY	MONDAY	TUESDAY	WEDNESDAY	THURSDAY	FRIDAY	SATURDAY

On the days you get to enjoy your me time, give yourself a high five! You can mark your calendar with a star, happy face, sticker, or any symbol you choose, to note that that was a day you took good care of yourself. Be mindful and aware of how many days in a row you prioritized you, because you're worth prioritizing every day!

Intense = Tense

In best-case scenarios, adrenaline gives you the fuel you need to accomplish something, unleash your maximum strength, and help you stay cognitively laser focused. In worst-case scenarios, adrenaline can cause mood swings, weight gain, headaches, increased heart rate, and sweating. When you feel adrenaline that stems from anxiety, you need to take that energy and channel it into focus and movement in order to remove yourself from danger or threats or protect yourself from it. If you aren't actually in any danger, then you can use progressive muscle relaxation to soothe those intense feelings that go hand in hand with adrenaline. When you tighten and release your muscles, your body will physically relax and let anxiety go. The more you practice this, the sharper you will be at this skill, and it can serve as an easy go-to when you need anxiety relief, helping you practice patience until those calmer feelings set in.

Progressive Muscle Relaxation: As you breathe in, you will tense and tighten an area while counting to 4. Then you will breathe out, releasing the tension and letting the muscle relax while counting to 4. You can do any of these sitting or standing—whatever feels comfortable.

Fists:

1. Breathe in 1, 2, 3, 4 and tighten your fists like you are going to punch someone.
2. Breathe out 1, 2, 3, 4 and release your fists.

Fists, elbows, arms:

1. Breathe in 1, 2, 3, 4; tighten your fists; and keep your elbows and arms in a L-shaped position, tight against your body.

2. Breathe out 1, 2, 3, 4 and release your fists, elbows, and arms.

Legs, knees, feet:

1. Breathe in 1, 2, 3, 4 while tightening your legs, pushing your knees and feet together, and squeezing your toes.
2. Breathe out 1, 2, 3, 4 and release your legs, knees, and feet.

Mindful Exercise

Fate is defined as a force outside your control that makes things happen. However, you also have free will and the ability to make choices that best serve you and your life. When you choose patience as a guide, you learn to trust yourself, and through this trust you can more easily accept what is happening in the moment, rather than worrying about what may be fated to happen. In moments that you need to navigate the rough waters, patience can help hold you steady.

1. When do you find that you lose patience with yourself?

_____

_____

2. List any feelings, emotions, and physical symptoms you experience when you are overwhelmed.

_____

_____

_____

_____

3. Check off the following ways you need to practice patience for yourself:

- ☐ slowing down
- ☐ intending to stay present
- ☐ identifying free time in my schedule
- ☐ using affirmations
- ☐ meditating and building calm
- ☐ other: _____

4. Going forward, how will you recognize when your anxiety is not being well managed?

_____

_____

5. How will you use patience as a guide to get back on track?

_____

_____

6. What do you need in order to let go of frustration, anger, annoyance, and sadness that you aren't moving fast enough through life?

_____

_____

MINDFUL MOMENT

The attitude of patience helps you persevere and stay calm. It is a skill that gives you the ability to pause and maintain control when feelings of frustration and anger tempt you to make snap decisions. Slowing down helps your brain make positive choices and set boundaries for yourself and others. Becoming aware of your impatient triggers will help you learn from your mistakes, develop methods to problem solve, and pay better attention to the life lessons in front of you. Slowing down will give you the chance to enjoy the unique and individual path you are on.

Anxiety can distort your thoughts, causing you to attempt to predict, fortune-tell, mind read, and catastrophize situations and experiences from an irrational and skewed perspective. When you feel overwhelmed, anxiety leans on these fear-based thoughts, but practicing patience will help break the patterns that cause you to rush and try, against your better interest, to stay two steps ahead. Being patient and slowing down gives you permission to stay present; it helps you enjoy each second, minute, and hour. Taking what you need to be successful and accepting the pace of your voyage each wave at a time will help you have empathy for yourself and others. Remember to prioritize your voyage and celebrate all you have learned along the way!

POSITIVE VIBES

"I have the patience for this moment today. Right now, this is exactly where I need to be. I will be kind to myself and trust the process of each moment. Rushing will only cause me to miss out on the present."

YOUR TAKEAWAYS

*"Sometimes things aren't clear right away.
That's where you need to be patient
and persevere and see where things lead."*

— Mary Pierce

→ Patience is the skill and attitude that helps you stay calm; it is the ability to pause, slow down, and thoughtfully push back against frustration and anger.

→ Anxiety might cause you to mind read, fortune-tell, and catastrophize a situation. The attitude of patience will provide the necessary wisdom to slow down and challenge these thoughts.

→ Expectations from yourself or others can leave you feeling overwhelmed and wanting to rush from one thing onto the next. When you do this, you are not fully present in your own life.

→ Building patience with yourself and others will help you strengthen your empathy muscle—the ability to understand and share emotions without judgment.

→ Prioritize yourself so you can develop patience as a practice to avoid being overwhelmed; when you are overwhelmed, you are less likely to stay present and in the moment.

Idea Questions

→ How will you practice patience with yourself? With others?

→ What will be the tool you use to slow down when you feel yourself rushing to the next thing?

→ How will patience help you be more compassionate to yourself and others?

→ Thinking of what you need to develop the attitude of patience, which exercise will you use this week?

CHAPTER SIX

TRUST IN YOURSELF

Stop the noise and tune in to yourself! Technology and society may attempt to dictate their version of who you are supposed to be through advertising on social media, websites, emails, billboards, videos, commercials, etc. Fun fact: It is estimated that in 2021, you were exposed to somewhere between 6,000 to 10,000 ads a day. Being bombarded with all of these messages can impact your self-esteem and overall identity of who you think you are supposed to be or become. Targeted advertisements tell you what clothes to buy, what tricked-out cell phone to use, and even where you should vacation. Being inundated with so many external messages can shape your level of trust within yourself and with others. Difficult emotions including anxiety, fear, and uncertainty can also cause you to question your sense of trust in yourself. In this chapter, you are going to strive for vulnerability; open yourself up and be honest about how you feel without judgment. On this leg of your journey, you'll learn where you mindfully need to build a stronger bond of trust in yourself.

THE MINDFUL WAY

Vulnerability is often thought of as a weakness, a point where something can break. Author Brené Brown, who has done extensive research on vulnerability, defines vulnerability as "uncertainty, risk, and emotional exposure." Being vulnerable is not about where you can break; it is about your inner strength, how to be courageous, and how to show up for situations and be seen. Vulnerability is the risk you take when you truly show yourself to the world because the risk is that you cannot control how people receive you or how they react to you when you are seen. What you can control is the trust within yourself—your ability to remain brave and be courageous. When you show up for yourself wholeheartedly, a door opens to build that trust. To do so, first you have to be honest and acknowledge your feelings, be attuned to your body, and pay attention to your needs.

There are many areas in life where you may be, or feel like, a stranger to yourself; there are things that you do subconsciously or without understanding why. Jon Kabat-Zinn describes the human body as "complex and beautiful." Think of your body—each day your body maintains the homeostasis of life, and you trust that your organs will function, your lungs will fill with air countless times, and your heart will beat 60 to 100 times a minute without your intervention. Most people take for granted all the amazing things their body can do, like walking, running, and jumping, and typically only tune in when their body is in pain, or when an injury occurs, and the freedom of normal physical functioning is taken away.

From your head to your toes, think of how ingeniously your body works and how all the different parts work together in harmony. When looking to build trust, the body is a great reference point; you know you can implicitly trust it to breathe, walk, and pump your heart. Your mind is just as complex and beautiful.

The same way that you trust in your body, you must trust in your relationships with yourself and with others. Trust in relationships begins with authenticity and vulnerability—it builds gradually. When you make decisions that have positive outcomes, those experiences enable you to move more easily on to the next situation with confidence. Slowly but surely, that sense of confidence helps you trust in yourself. Another way to think of this is to consider qualities or feelings you possess that you know you can rely on, such as the love you have for your family. Even in moments that you might not get along, you know you love your family and, even better, that that love has taught you that being vulnerable to offer love to someone is a worthwhile risk. Once you identify these areas that you can be vulnerable in, you will be able to build a stronger sense of trust.

In order to best understand trust and why it's such an important part of being mindful, especially in the face of anxiety, you need to also understand distrust. Distrust is felt when you cannot rely on someone and feel suspicious or doubtful of their words, actions, or intentions. In moments of feeling distrust, you can remind yourself of concrete reasons that you can trust in someone and make a shift in your mindset. It's important to stay present and be mindful of the story you tell yourself about what it means to be trusting. If you're struggling with trust in any relationship, are you perhaps thinking about past fears? Fear—of being lied to, of being vulnerable without receiving care, etc.—can hold you back and cause an overreaction, such as distrust. Remember to stay vulnerable in your interactions and take what you need to allow self-love, self-compassion, and respect. Keep yourself accountable for your needs; feeling safe and secure will help overcome distrust, helping you be your best self, the person who has good intentions for themselves and their relationships. Use the insight you have developed throughout this workbook to meet distrust at the door before it walks through and influences how you feel.

Think about how far you have come on this journey, how well you've tackled challenging topics. Through all your hard work, wisdom, and self-growth, you can and will encourage trust within yourself, and trusting yourself will better help you trust others. Remember, trust is a practice, and you can build your practice moment by moment, and eventually your life will be full of positive healthy relationships and your circle of trust will be that much stronger.

COMMON ANXIETY PATTERNS

Anxiety breaks your trust with yourself and your relationships, thereby harming your most important and loving connections. When fear is in charge and leading the way, you are less likely to live in the present moment, which makes it hard to enjoy things as they are and reassure yourself that you are safe and able to trust. Anxiety patterns are a diversion from the present; they question your confidence and what you know; building trust will put you on track, easing your mind from developing the questions in the first place.

Personalization

Personalization is a cognitive distortion that occurs when you take things personally even though they're not actually connected to you or even caused by you. You become the main character of every story and relate all things to yourself; this creates feelings that lead to shame and inappropriate guilt. Imagine that you're at a birthday party, but no one is talking to you and you're standing alone. In this situation, you might begin to think that your friends don't like you, or the only reason they invited you was because they felt sorry for you. Here is where shame invades your brain space, leaving you feeling like a charity case rather than someone who is loved and wanted. The reality could simply be that you went to get a drink and something to eat, which meant exiting the conversation briefly, rather than actually being excluded. And more important, you *were* invited to the party, because your friends like and value you.

With personalization, despite the many variables of a situation, you solely burden yourself with the blame, assuming you are and must be at fault, even if the situation is far beyond your control. Imagine that you were 10 minutes late to a movie because you couldn't find parking, and you immediately assumed that your friends were annoyed with you and having a terrible time as a result. In reality, they knew you were running late because you texted them, they were pleased to know you weren't hurt or sick, and they happily watched the previews and ate popcorn until you arrived. Personalization can make you feel like you are directly being attacked, excluded, or targeted by those around you even though there isn't any proof of that being the case. It's your anxiety that falsely feeds you the narrative that you are at fault for anything that goes wrong, even when that is so rarely, if ever, the truth.

Blaming

Blaming is when you rigidly assign responsibility to others for what went wrong in a situation. It's almost the opposite of personalization in that it intensely places the shame and guilt on other people. In turn, you don't take responsibility for your actions and assume the role of a victim who can blame others for their pain. Rather than reflecting on what happened, what was said, or the feelings you feel, you identify a scapegoat for the situation and shift any blame onto them. What's worse is that this cognitive distortion can convince you that others are hurting you on purpose. You might tell yourself, "They *always* make me feel bad" or "I'm not good enough." The reality, however, is that you control how you feel, and no one has the power to make you feel bad. Blaming means you do not have to be vulnerable and honest with your feelings—it might protect you from taking any responsibility, but it isn't a fair, healthy, or honest way to look at things.

Pleasing

Pleasing can come from a combination of your anxious thoughts and poor boundaries where you feel responsible for everyone's happiness, prioritizing it above your own and acting as a people pleaser. Holding yourself responsible for everyone's emotions is a heavy load to carry. Pleasing others often means that your emotions and needs are being ignored, which makes you develop distrust within yourself. Your anxiety grows stronger through avoiding dealing with what is really happening. You may say "yes" to things you do not want to do or commit yourself to helping when you do not have the capacity. Maybe your family asked you for help with making dinner and even though you have to get a big homework assignment done, you want to please them and said "yes." But now that you're helping them, you can't get your homework done, and feel that they were selfish or unkind for asking for help at all. What's worse is if pleasing makes you tell yourself, "This is why you always get low grades, because you're always helping everyone else!" What would be more helpful in this situation would be to establish boundaries, based on your emotions or your bandwidth, say "no" when you need to but also hold yourself accountable for your actions. When you hold yourself accountable—such as recognizing that you caved to pleasing rather than prioritizing your needs—it makes you be that much more vulnerable and therefore honest with yourself. By identifying and confronting these feelings of fear and anxiety, you can build the trust that you need and deserve.

REAL TALK

Kirra was a bright student who was creative, had boundless energy, and was an avid ice-skater. I used to joke that she would become a CEO one day because of all of her talents: she was artistic, athletic, outspoken, and high achieving. One day, Kirra came into my office in tears holding a math test with a very low score. Regardless of her test score, I still saw Kirra as the bright shining star that she was, standing in front of me, but in that moment, she viewed herself differently. Kirra cried and said, "I got an F! I practiced, I studied, I did everything I was supposed to, but I'm so anxious, and my anxiety just gets in the way." I offered her a tissue and said, "One test does not define you, Kirra."

In that moment, Kirra's anxiety had written a narrative that said she was always going to be bad at math, even though she was consistently a top student. I asked her, "Kirra, who is telling you that you are bad at math?" She looked up, a little confused, and said, "This test, my grade, obviously!" I laughed and said, "Do tests and grades talk? Are they online now, too? What's their handle?" Kirra rolled her eyes and told me she knew what I meant was that she wasn't trusting herself or her skill level. The issue was not that she was not capable; it was that she didn't believe she was capable.

I told Kirra to think about what it was like when she would ice-skate. "How are you able to do jumps and spins on such a thin blade?" She responded lightly, "I use my balance and my core, plus I'm pretty flexible." I reminded Kirra that just like she relied on herself not to fall on the ice, she could rely on her emotions and mind in the same way when it came to math. Kirra let it sink in for a minute. "I never thought of it like that. When I skate, I feel the ice and tell myself, I want to go backward and jump, and my body just does it." Kirra stood up and said, "I can go backward on the ice, and I can do math!"

Like Kirra, you have a narrative that you tell yourself—sometimes it stems from a place of anxiety or distrust, and other times from a place of confidence and trust. Trusting yourself may feel challenging, but remind yourself that you are trustworthy.

Trust Your Body

To trust others, you must first trust yourself. When you wake up each day, you can trust that your body will take care of you. Think of how your lungs and heart work together, inhaling oxygen and processing it as you breathe out without even thinking about it. If you had to remember to breathe, that would be a real challenge—think of how many times you forget where you put your phone! For this meditation, you will lean into trusting your body, paying attention to how remarkable it truly is and how special you are.

1. Find a quiet space, free of distraction, to lie down or sit down, whatever is most comfortable for you. If you lie down, the goal is to be present and not give in to sleep.
2. Take a few deep breaths at your own pace.
3. Scan your body from your head to your toes. If you notice any aches or discomfort, remember that this is your body's way of sending you a message, reminding you that you need to care for it and not take it for granted.
4. Take in a deep breath and let any discomfort leave your body.
5. Tell your body, "I understand you need attention, and today, in this moment, I see you for all you give to me."
6. Take a deep breath and feel how it fills you with trust.
7. Pause for a moment. Breathe in all that you have and are grateful for, and exhale worry and stress.
8. As your body takes in air, feel how it is taking care of you right now in this moment.
9. Scan your body once more with an awareness of what you feel.
10. Thank your body for taking care of you each day, in all the ways big and small, that it does.

Define It

Trust is not something you can touch; rather it is an attitude that is attached to your emotions. When you trust yourself, you can do things without judging yourself and accept you for exactly who you are. The first step to doing this is to define trust for yourself—use the following questions to guide your unique definition of trust.

What qualities do you look for in a friend that you trust?

☐ Authentic   ☐ A good listener
☐ Humble   ☐ Supportive
☐ Has integrity   ☐ Reflective
☐ Resourceful   ☐ Selfless
☐ Kind   ☐ Other: _____
☐ Compassionate   ☐ Other: _____

What actions can someone do to help you trust them?

_____

_____

_____

What are a few behaviors that cause you to question someone's trustworthiness?

_____

_____

_____

How do you know you trust someone?

_____

_____

_____

When you feel close to someone, what thoughts, feelings, or secrets do you share with them?

_____

_____

_____

Now you'll create your own definition of trust using your responses to the questions you answered.

Trust for me is: _____

I trust those who have the following:

Qualities: _____

Actions: _____

Behaviors: _____

Reflect: What do you need in order to better trust yourself?

Qualities:

_____

_____

_____

Actions:

_____

_____

_____

Behaviors:

_____

_____

_____

Hold the Line

Boundaries are limits you use to create a healthy sense of space both physically and emotionally. These healthy limitations help you understand the differences between want, need, and desire, both for yourself personally and with others. Your limits can vary based on the day and the situation, but mindfulness can focus your attention on when you need boundaries emotionally, physically, psychologically, or even spiritually. When you recognize that there is discomfort in any of these areas and you trust your assessment of those feelings, you can also realize that you are worth holding the line.

Physically, you may be standing in line and someone's shopping cart is right up against you. You may move forward to create more comfortable space or politely ask them for a bit more room. Boundary!

Psychologically, you may see your phone light up with a text from someone who will surely distract you from your homework. Your brain says, "I need to focus," so you put the phone on silent mode and turn it upside down. Boundary!

Emotionally, your friend may ask for your help resolving an issue they are having. But if they are only interested in complaining, or talking poorly about another person, or ignoring your advice to solve the problem, you can tell them, "Hey, it seems like this is really hard for you. When you are ready to find the solution, I will be here for you." Boundary!

Mindfulness brings attention to your emotions and physical self. Trust your body and mind when they let you know they need a limit.

Reflect: What is one boundary that you need to put into place to support your own well-being?

_____

_____

Take a Bite

Eating mindfully—which means focusing on what food you eat and what it provides to you—can support your body, your mind, and your relationship with food. Reflecting mindfully on how and when you eat is a great step forward in trusting yourself. Here are a couple of mindful tricks you can use:

Eat without screens. When you eat in front of a screen (such as a TV, tablet, or phone) your mind is focused elsewhere and you are not aware of how much or how fast you are eating.

Eat in an area free of work or clutter. If you aren't distracted by the space that you are eating in, you will be better able to use your senses to eat mindfully. What does the food smell like? Taste like? What is its relative temperature? What colors do you see?

Always eat off a plate or from a bowl. When you eat out of a container or a bag, it's much harder to measure out portions, which prevents you from being present in the moment when eating.

Take one bite at a time. Taking one bite at a time that comfortably fits in your mouth will help you eat slowly, thus helping your body digest and be happy. Anxiety can cause us to eat faster, so it's important to be mindful of your emotions with each bite.

Your emotions can cause you to develop a relationship with food that often questions your level of trust. You may indulge in snacks or comfort food when you are stressed (chips, candy, cookies—these are my favorites when stressed). Being aware of your anxiety when you are eating will help balance your food intake, leading to overall healthier habits. Eating a few cookies is good, whereas eating the entire box, due to feeling anxious, isn't great for your overall health. You can use these "Take a Bite" rules to make small shifts. Each positive choice you make will add to your trust jar, each moment filling it to help develop trust in yourself and your food choices.

YOU'VE GOT THIS!

On your journey you may come across a few road signs: one lane ahead, work zone, road closed, etc. The process of trusting in yourself can also come with some of its own signs, like you have been on this road before, you were successful the last time you did this, you got this. With mindfulness, you can reflect on where you feel comfortable going and challenge yourself to build trust where the road detours. It may be scary, and you can handle what is ahead.

Affirmation: *"The person I trust today is me. Each day my trust is strengthened, helping me in turn trust others."*

Recharge

When you feel drained and are running on empty, making life choices and staying present can feel difficult and cause distrust. You may question your actions, feelings, and thoughts. Practicing self-care—when you take action to care for your physical, emotional, or mental health with positive actions and words—is a great way to recharge and refill your energy tank. Below are 20 quick self-care things you can do for yourself when you are feeling stressed or anxious, plus empty space for you to add any other things that help you recharge.

☐ Drink hot tea ☐ Eat healthily ☐ Compliment yourself

☐ Listen to music ☐ Go outside ☐ Read

☐ Exercise ☐ Dance ☐ Meditate

☐ Go for a walk ☐ Hug yourself ☐ _____

☐ Take a nap ☐ Breathe ☐ _____

☐ Write a gratitude list ☐ Plan a fun activity ☐ _____

☐ Sing ☐ _____

☐ Cuddle your pet ☐ Drink water ☐ _____

☐ Journal ☐ Take a break ☐ _____

Reflect:

→ What does your mind and body need to recharge?

_____

_____

_____

→ When can you fit your self-care/recharge activity into your day?

_____

_____

_____

→ How can you make one or more of these a daily practice?

_____

_____

_____

Not My Circus, Not My Monkeys

Negative self-talk can impact anyone. Everyone has had a moment of doubt, a time when their inner critic is speaking loudly and obnoxiously. Listening to these messages can shake your confidence and limit your full potential. Additionally, you might hear external negative messaging that you are not enough, or you are bad at something, from someone else, and even if you know it isn't true, hearing something enough can trick you into thinking it's the truth.

   In this exercise you are going to be honest and vulnerable with yourself; you'll acknowledge any statements, critiques, or harsh comments you have heard. To do this you need to trust in the process of being uncomfortable to ultimately feel more comfortable. You got this!

1. Find a space where you feel psychologically safe and supported; it may be your room, a quiet corner, or under a tree.
2. Take a few breaths, a quick pause, or a quiet moment to recenter yourself if you need before you begin. If any discomfort comes up, recognize the feeling without judgment.
3. Get a piece of blank or lined paper, a pen or pencil, and a timer (you can use your watch or phone). Think of all the negative messages that you have told yourself, set a timer for two minutes, and write them down until the timer goes off. Whatever emotion comes up, whether it's fury or sadness, let it give you energy to write.
4. When the timer goes off after two minutes, take the paper and fold it up as tightly as you can.
5. Take a deep breath in and out.
6. Repeat the following statement aloud: *"These messages do not define me; they are not my monkeys! I am patient, nonjudgmental, and open-minded. My path is mine to make, and I trust myself to learn the way forward with each moment, each step. I may stumble along the way, but I will withstand this storm."*
7. Now throw away the paper!

Trust Me

Complete the following statements as a way to reflect and hold yourself accountable. You can also use these as reminders to show how much progress you have made.

I notice my anxiety impact my trust level with myself when . . .

_____

My top three strengths are . . .

_____

_____

_____

One thing I learned about myself this week/month is . . .

_____

I plan to learn to trust myself more by . . .

_____

I need to be flexible with myself with . . .

_____

MINDFUL MOMENT

Anxiety can cause you to question your sense of stability within yourself and your relationships. It can sneak fear into areas of your life where security and safety should exist. Using the practice of trust will help make stronger bonds between yourself and others. With each day that passes that bond of trust will grow, lessening the noises that come from cognitive distortions like blaming and personalization. When you trust yourself, you'll be better able to take care of your body and your mind. When you silence your inner self-critic and any negative external messages and center the perspective on yourself and the positive things you do, trust is possible! Giving yourself the attention and care you need will grow self-compassion, self-trust, self-love, and self-respect.

Trusting in yourself will be the catalyst for trusting others and furthering your relationships. Recharge yourself so you have the bandwidth to give to yourself and others. When you overextend yourself, it can lead to anxiety and resentment. Establish the boundaries you need to feel balance in yourself and balance in your relationships. You set the pace, so be flexible with yourself if you stumble. Remember, everyone stumbles, but when you do stumble, you can pick yourself back up and use the tools from this workbook to step forward.

POSITIVE VIBES

Anxiety can make you question yourself and foster distrust. When you feel this happening, let the thought know that you hear it. Then, tell yourself the following:

"I bring attention to what I need in this moment.
I am taking a step forward and trusting myself.
I believe I can and so I will with a little flair."

YOUR TAKEAWAYS

"Self-trust is the first secret of success."

—Ralph Waldo Emerson

→ Anxiety can make you question the trust you have in yourself and others.

→ Personalization can distort your thinking. If you become the main character in every story, it will make the situation about you in a negative way that is often divorced from reality.

→ Blaming, or when you assign responsibility to someone else without acknowledging your contribution, is also a type of distorted thinking.

→ You are not defined by the anxious messages you have received from yourself, others, or society that try to tell you that you are less than. You are enough.

→ Running on empty creates distrust; being fully charged helps cultivate self-trust.

→ Self-care supports your physical, emotional, and mental health, and it's helpful to have a recharge plan.

→ Boundaries hold a healthy line for you and your relationships. When you feel uncomfortable, taken advantage of, or overwhelmed, assert a boundary with confidence.

Idea Questions

→ How will you practice self-trust this week?

→ When your anxious thoughts try to suggest that you're at fault for things outside your control, how will you pause and assert yourself to build trust?

→ What is one boundary that you need to trust yourself or others?

→ What resonated the most for you from this chapter?

CHAPTER SEVEN

BE IN THE MOMENT

Your goal . . . is no goal! Wait, what? Yes, no goal. Tug-of-war may be a game played on field day, but it is also a game you play in your mind: the push and pull between ideas, goals, thoughts, relationships, answers on a test, what to post, etc. In this chapter, let's work on shifting your mindset away from success and learn non-striving, which may seem odd, because setting goals helps you achieve your vision. But non-striving can be helpful, because not everything needs a finite line where you can reach the "enough" mark. Life continues—appreciating the moment can free you from the pressure of constantly having a finish line. Mindfulness is a practice where you develop awareness in observation. You see things openly without judgment and accept the here and now. Trusting that you are enough regardless of a goal or success will be how you practice non-striving.

THE MINDFUL WAY

So many people grow up trained to work for awards, trophies, and victory. Winning becomes a theme song through setting goals, achieving, learning that new trick or new play, getting to the next level on a game, having a certain number of followers, or being competitive until success is attained. Striving is ingrained in daily life. Non-striving, on the other hand, is living moment to moment without any agenda. Developing a non-striving attitude is extremely unusual as people are always going somewhere and doing something. So, how does one develop awareness on non-doing and just being? Let's look to the Chinese philosophy of wu wei. In Chinese, "wu wei" means "doing nothing" or "non-doing." The Dao De Jing (Daoist scripture) refers to this concept as "The Way never acts yet nothing is left undone."

Living with a non-striving attitude releases you from trying to get to a better moment or escape from your past and allows you to stay present in this moment without working to make anything different happen. It is the awareness to nonjudgmentally let things be as they are. Here is the hard part: Everyone has a to-do list, so this seems counterproductive. Non-striving is not being lazy; it means you are not forcing a goal or finish line in the moment. Jon Kabat-Zinn teaches that to keep balance within your to-do list, as long as it may be, you need to recharge, nurture, and heal yourself. If you can match your to-do list with a non-striving attitude, you will be able to get more things accomplished, because you will have the energy from recharging. Non-striving helps you have self-care, self-compassion, and healing from all that you give to the world. It is a way to invest in yourself and to refill your batteries cognitively, emotionally, and physically. When you are 100 percent recharged, you function at a higher level. If you are truly honest, your to-do lists do not usually include a sufficient recharge plan. You have to build the intention to be, rather than just do all the time. When you rest and refuel, you will be more productive.

When you are rested, relaxed, and recharged, your mind and body have the capacity for greater wisdom. You are a better thinker and solution finder, and you are more emotionally regulated when you have the space to just be. As you practice non-striving throughout this chapter, notice how when you let go of striving for specific outcomes, the achievement of your goals naturally falls into place. The shift in focus allows you to see and accept each moment by moment. Jon Kabat-Zinn teaches that, in time, progression toward your goals will happen as you strive to non-strive.

COMMON ANXIETY PATTERNS

Anxiety can get in the way of non-striving because when anxiety shows up, you seek control. You want to fix, label, ship, box, etc. so you can create order. You exert cognitive labor striving for control. Cognitive labor is when you are anticipating needs, making decisions, figuring out how to box and ship, and then you check on how all these things are going.

Adrenaline + Anxiety

Your body makes adrenaline when you feel anxious. Adrenaline puts a lot of pressure on your central nervous system, causing headaches, confusion, difficulty sleeping, diarrhea, frequent urination, restlessness, changes in your eating (more food or less food), tearfulness, and other problems. Adrenaline and anxiety can have positive benefits such as pushing you to do things you are uncomfortable with, knocking out that to-do list, moving to the next goal, the next task, the next achievement, the next job, the next event, the next award. It can keep you feeling invincible! I call this "Ready, Fire, Set, Go!" Let's look at an example.

Ready, Fire, Set, Go!

Imagine you are given a project and you are "ready"; your mind "fires" ideas, solutions, ways to get the project finished. You "set" a goal to accomplish the project and you "go" do it in rock-star-status time. When you function in this model, it feels like a fun time and you can get so much accomplished. People may praise you for your ambition and your fast-paced work. It is like you are sprinting to success!

When you have adrenaline anxiety, every time you cross the finish line it becomes a little less exciting, and you strive for more. Strive to check tasks off the to-do list. Strive for more recognition, awards, honors, and accolades to your name. The struggle with being in this striving state of mind and thought loop is that it is never enough, and you are moving on to the next thing, never in the moment of here and now. You can be sitting ready to receive your award and your mind is thinking about what your next goal should be. You may have 100 likes on your photo, and you begin to worry about what you are going to post next.

Cortisol + Anxiety

Remember Aesop's fable of "The Tortoise and the Hare"? Children are warned that the very confident hare ran so fast, he felt like he could take a nap, while the slow-moving yet determined tortoise kept pace and won the race. The moral of the story was that when you keep pace and are emotionally regulated, you will be more successful than when moving too quickly and not being emotionally regulated. When you move too fast, you become careless and make mistakes, which can hurt you, your relationships, and your future. Cortisol is created in your body when you are anxious, and like the hare, it has another agenda. While the hare thought he was okay, your adrenaline has you feeling great until your body produces and builds too much cortisol. Over time, cortisol can create migraines, stomach issues, and heart disease.

Non-striving as a practice will help you personify the tortoise's pace, allowing you to enjoy your life one mile marker at a time. You are able to slow down and stay present to appreciate the moment in front of you. Non-striving will help create awareness that life is happening all around you, and to see it, you need only look up and be present. When you strive and strive, you miss out on your relationships and experiences. You overlook the steps, the mile markers, the people helping you succeed. Take a deep breath when you feel yourself on the striving loop; it can feel like a hamster wheel!

REAL TALK

Ethan was a full-of-life person. His charismatic personality helped him become president of his class. While we were taking a walk around the track, talking, Ethan said, "I just want to be at the top and fit it all in." I looked back and I said, "Me too! Problem is we only get twenty-four hours a day, and sleep is essential." We both started laughing. Ethan said, "I just feel like when I accomplish this or achieve that goal, what's next? I can do more! I can go after something bigger; you know?" He continued to describe the pressure of collecting awards and achievements, because he felt like he was on fire and needed to keep it burning. I told Ethan I could also relate to that feeling, like what is the next thing for me to achieve, and it was a game against myself. That game we talked about starts and stops with us. Sometimes we have to just be to be without always having a mile marker tell us how far we have come. I asked Ethan, "How many laps have we taken on the track now?" He looked around and smiled, "I have no clue! Was I supposed to be counting?" I said, "No. Because I am so fun, you never thought to count the laps, right? Together we are walking and talking, without a goal. We are walking and talking to discuss things." Ethan thoughtfully looked up at the sky, and said, "I always have an agenda to work toward. I never thought about just doing something just to do it. Weird."

Ethan is not alone. Most people have a deadline, finish line, and/or goal-oriented agenda. Being in that moment on the track and being mindful of being in the moment helped Ethan realize the walk was important regardless of the conclusion. Mindfulness can help you be in the moment and enjoy the now without parameters. With non-striving you can walk and enjoy each other's company and learn from each other without the burden of reaching a certain number of steps forward.

I Am Enough

Throughout this meditation, keep the intention of "I am enough" in mind.

1. Get into a seated posture on the floor or in a chair.
2. Settle in so that your legs and back feel straight.
3. Take a deep breath in and out.
4. Read the following statements out loud, one by one, and really let their meaning settle in with you.

"There is so much happening, sitting here is enough."
"Nothing has to happen because so much is already happening."
"I am free from fixing things right now."
"I am breathing without having to do it intentionally."
"My body will keep moving and filling my lungs full of air and life."
"I am here breathing in and out."
"Sounds and noises are happening without any effort from me."
"They were happening before I sat down; sounds are just happening."
"I do not have to do anything to hear the sounds I hear."
"The sounds may dance around me and come and go."
"Notice the sounds. I am listening."
"I have no agenda even though the sounds are moving around me."
"Thoughts and judgments are just happening, and they have their own agenda."
"As thoughts and judgments come, I just observe them."
"I do not have to do anything. If I feel the need to change or strive, I will just observe and stay present."
"Reading the words on this page is enough."
"Sitting here is enough. I am enough."

5. Now take a deep breath in and out. Stand up and know that you are enough. You can release yourself from involving yourself in everything.

Walk It Out

When you take a walk, there is usually a destination in mind. Your goal is typically to get from point A to point B. When you set the intention to be non-striving, it takes patience to "do" without that idea of a goal.

In this exercise you are going to take a walk with the intention of enjoying the view.

→ If you come across a friendly face, maybe say "Hello."

→ Take in all the nature you see, or the cityscape.

→ Notice how interesting your path is without the goal of finding anything along the way.

→ Be mindful of your emotions and how your body feels.

→ When you think of your goal, take a deep breath and free yourself from that finish line.

Be in the moment, feel the wind, hear it in the trees or whistling down the street. Watch a leaf sway or a squirrel run around. Just be in the moment on this path you have set; walk out the goal and destination. Detach and discover the attitude of non-doing one step at a time!

Invisible Ink

Names are an example of not doing. You probably write your name at the top of your test or homework without thinking too much about it. It's just what you do! You are going to keep practicing this attitude of not doing by essentially doing what you do every day, but now you will do it in the air. You are not going to be concerned or judge yourself on neatness, as you will be using invisible ink.

1. Ball your hands tight like a fist and release. Repeat two times.
2. Stretch out your hands and fingers as wide as you can make them, forcing your thumb and pinky as far apart as possible.
3. Wiggle your fingers like jazz or dance hands, however feels the most comfortable.
4. Take your right hand and draw your first name in the air using cursive or printing.
5. Do this a few times and just observe to see if you can see each letter and your name, watching each letter string together as you write in the air. Observe how the shapes of the letters come together.

My right hand in the air made:

6. Take your left hand and draw your last name in the air using cursive or printing.
7. Do this also a few times and just observe to see if this hand was harder or the same as the right hand considering neither had tangible pen and paper.

My left hand in the air made:

Stevens

Without trying to be neat or concerned about your handwriting, you were able to just write your name without the baggage of stress and anxiety. Imagination can connect us to understand our feelings and emotions. When you are feeling your "to-do" list grow into a long scary monster, pause and write your name in the air.

Put It in Writing

Ideas, thoughts, feelings flow through your mind like water. Each droplet can connect to the next creating a stream. The more you allow the stream to grow, the bigger it will become and eventually it can turn into a river. Writing has the same energy connecting one idea to the next. For this exercise, you will need a paper and pen. You are going to extract your ideas, thoughts, and feelings and journal them below without a time marker, without a word count. Just allow your thoughts and ideas to leave your pen. If you feel a block, write any words that come to mind or scribble and draw until you feel ready to transfer and convert yourself to paper. Free-flowing thoughts do not hold judgment; they embody patience and acceptance. Allow yourself to just be and write.

YOU'VE GOT THIS!

"Don't confuse motion and progress. A rocking horse keeps moving but doesn't make any progress."

– Alfred Armand Montapert

Striving to non-strive takes patience and practice. Welcome your path without a destination and move as you feel comfortable. Mindfully allow time to move without watching the clock. Enjoy the moment; progress is inevitable.

Squirrel

Modern technology provides the possibility for thousands of distractions. Your phone, watch, and computer notifications keep you engaged at a level that is bananas. You need to ensure that they do not pop up and trigger you to strive on and have your brain yell, "What's that! Look this up! Idea!" Your brain craves information. Your brain cells fire up and make connections to your technology. Dopamine is released, triggering feelings of a reward when those cells fire up, which in turn stimulates learning. You cannot get into flow or wu wei if your brain is anxious and wanting to move to the next better moment.

Take three minutes to list all your anxious triggers that force you to feel the need to strive. Keep in mind anything that breaks your concentration. It could be your messages making a noise, your alarm going off as a timer, your email flashing across your screen. Anything that takes you to focus on the next moment and ignore the here and now.

Anxious Triggers:

_____

_____

_____

_____

_____

Ready Yourself: Get what you need to be successful and recharged to stay in this moment.

☐ snack ☐ _____

☐ water ☐ _____

Reflect: What do you need to clear your mind and just be in this moment?

_____

_____

_____

_____

_____

Take a deep breath in and out. When you feel yourself drift off, politely bring yourself back to the moment. Observe your distractions or triggers. Accept them and remind yourself to engage with yourself and those you value.

The Power of Hugs

National Hugging Day is January 21 and was created by Rev. Kevin Zaborney in Michigan. He felt Americans were embarrassed to show their feelings and connect with others in public. Established between the winter holiday season and Valentine's Day, Reverend Zaborney hoped a day of hugging would support a time when most people experience an emotional low. Hugging releases oxytocin, helping you feel safe and less threatened. Your body responds less aggressively when you have higher levels of oxytocin; this helps reduce your fight-or-flight response, thus having you present in the moment and not waiting for the next.

According to research, receiving and giving a hug three or four times a day can promote significantly higher levels of well-being, mitigate stress, lower depression, lower heart disease, and even lower symptoms of a common cold! As you practice non-striving, hugging can support you reaching your goals without doing. Be intentional with those you love and people in your life who need permission to show their feelings. Hug those you feel comfortable with, as everyone has a need to feel safe and less stressed.

Hug a friend.
Hug a family member.
Hug someone who needs a hug.
Hug yourself.

Sending you a telepathic hug from this page right now!

Ask Yourself

1. Anxiety can have you feeling like you are going through the motions without going forward. When do you feel yourself going through the motions?

_____

_____

2. On your mindfulness quest, have you felt yourself striving to the next moment?

☐ Yes   ☐ Not sure

☐ Sometimes   ☐ No

3. What are the warning signs or triggers that make you focus on striving?

_____

_____

4. I have felt the most balance between doing and non-doing when . . .

_____

_____

5. List three things you need to feel recharged.

_____

_____

Reflect: Building in a recharge moment each day will keep you more grounded in the present. Make the commitment to yourself and add an activity each day to the chart below. Examples may be any of the exercises in this workbook, walking, coloring, listening to music, reading solely for pleasure, and doing nothing at all.

SUNDAY	MONDAY	TUESDAY	WEDNESDAY	THURSDAY	FRIDAY	SATURDAY

MINDFUL MOMENT

Your striving thoughts can make you feel like you are on fire and your actions feel invincible. Feeling invincible feels amazing; however, at some point you crash and burn out of exhaustion. Adrenaline anxiety can be powerful, and cortisol can be the backlash on your body. You can feel that you are not enough and achieving your next trophy will be the answer for you to be worth it. Be mindful of your anxiety triggers that fuel the fire. Be kind to yourself and do not resort to shame. Your relationships and experiences do not have a finish line; they have a flexible path. As your path diverges, turn and grow. The path will continue on as you grow yourself and your relationships. Be an active participant in the here and now. You can develop a mindset of non-striving and accept that the world will continue on and be all around you even when you slow down. In the present moment, you will learn openly, begin to see and accept without judgment. Slowing down does not mean that you are lazy or not willing to do the work. It means you are willing to persevere and go the distance! Embrace the present and all it has to teach you, and invest in yourself and the people who also choose to invest in you. You are worth the time and energy to be with each moment of each day!

POSITIVE VIBES

When you feel yourself moving without progress . . . hit Pause. Wrap your arms around yourself and repeat the following:

"I was enough yesterday.
I am enough today.
I will be enough tomorrow."

YOUR TAKEAWAYS

"Now and then, it's good to pause in our pursuit of happiness and just be happy."

— Guillaume Apollinaire

→ Non-striving frees you from escaping or avoiding and allows for you to be in the moment without the urgency to leave. The attitude of non-doing eases you to stay present from moment to moment, without working to make anything different happen.

→ Striving keeps you hostage to not feeling enough and moving on to the next best moment.

→ Know your triggers and what fosters your hamster wheel of striving.

→ You are enough! The "enough" mark does not exist. You are meant to be who you are right now.

→ Recharge your batteries cognitively, emotionally, and physically. When you are 100 percent recharged, the goals will come naturally with you present along the way.

Idea Questions

→ How will you practice non-striving this week?

→ When you feel yourself moving on to the next moment, the next to-do list item, how will you take a tortoise approach?

→ What is one strategy you will use to practice non-striving?

→ What was your aha moment in this chapter where you thought, "Hey, that's me"?

CHAPTER EIGHT

LET IT GO

Going from childhood to your teens means making new friends, attending new schools, and meeting new teachers. Your feet have grown, and you've let go of the old sneakers and embraced the new ones. When you let your sneakers go, the memories, the miles, and four-square games are still a part of who you have become today. You have been resilient in changing sneakers and schools; your feelings and thoughts are not always as easy. Your feelings, thoughts, and memories can follow patterns that can be unhelpful as they push and pull, and sometimes the struggle divides you and you feel conflicted. Anxiety can push away good things such as change and transition, and you may try to hold on tight and not let go. Mindfully letting go will help you move forward, opening a door of freedom to let you become the amazing person you are meant to be in this moment.

THE MINDFUL WAY

Each night, when you go to sleep, you let go and give in to relaxation and dreams. You release control and let your body recharge so you can wake up energized. You let go of holding on to staying awake and connected to your active life. When you are awake, it is much harder to let go. You cling to ideas and push away things that are uncomfortable. Your desires hold you captive, and letting go can feel like you are quitting, like you gave up. You hold on to things, possessions, thoughts, and ideas. You can get caught up in the way things should be, and you have an idea of how they should look. You become caught in a catch-and-release cycle. You have to build awareness when you get caught by your own wants and desires. Freedom exists when you open the door and let go. When you let go, you can reclaim your life and be open to the opportunity of change.

Marie Kondo, a bestselling author, a tidying genius, the star of her own hit Netflix show, and one of *Time* magazine's 100 Most Influential People in the World, developed a system of organization called the KonMari Method™. The goal is that you choose what you keep and keep only the things that spark joy for you. You thank the other items for taking care of you, and you let them go for someone else to enjoy. The KonMari Method tidies up clothes, books, papers, kimono (miscellaneous items), and sentimental items in a sequential way that is most comfortable emotionally. People all around the world are drawn to Marie Kondo because of her success and the importance of mindfulness. She teaches awareness of the feelings you attach to objects, especially around items someone gave to you and the meaning behind the gift. When you let go of sentimental items, the connection is not lost because you still have the memory.

The KonMari Method releases the emotional hold over belongings and clutter. It is helpful to tidy your thoughts and organize them like you would your dresser or desk. You need to create space to be creative! Think of your homework or loose notes—do you keep them, push them aside, or pile them up? When you keep all these things, they can grow into a giant clutter monster of overwhelm. Your thoughts are the same; they can pile up and create a push and pull for you. You can get stuck in your ways of thinking and have preconceived notions on how things should be, who you ought to be, who others should be. When you let go, you can reclaim your life.

You can reach these goals by simplifying your approach to everyday activities and encounters by creating space for what matters. When small things irritate you, let it go. Do not keep that irritating moment or repeat. When you make a mistake, letting go will release the shame and guilt and leave room for you to discover a lesson learned. Letting go is a powerful way to redirect your thoughts and release you from the pain of being chained down by them. Throughout this chapter, reflect on the emotions, feelings, and thoughts that are weighing you down. Slowly, set them free so you can be present on each page!

COMMON ANXIETY PATTERNS

Anxiety can have you hold on to fear, frustration, anger, thoughts, notions, ideas of how things should be and ought to be, and what perfect looks like, all of which limit you from your full potential. The narrative you tell yourself begins to shape your reality. It puts pressure on you and on your relationships. Your mind gets caught up in and trapped by what you hold on to and grasp; this pattern can then lead to your thoughts becoming habits. Often one thought will trigger another, and you begin to spiral down to a dark place with your obsessive and excessive thinking.

Narrative

Every day you tell yourself stories with regards to routine activities and observations. The narrations occur about what is happening in your life, what you are feeling, why you feel that way, and even about what is happening in the lives of others, or what other people are thinking. Your experiences shape these narratives, how you see the world, a situation, or a relationship. Your perspective is your perspective, uniquely created by how your brain receives information and deciphers it to interpret the facts and sifts how you are engaging in your life. Anxiety creates a filter on that narrative. One narrative you may tell yourself is that your anxiety prevents you from achieving success. You may feel that it can never be managed. But another perspective is that anxiety can push you to challenge yourself and that you have learned many aspects about yourself you would not have if you did not have anxiety. Anxiety can also be a positive force that helps you get stuff accomplished! Adrenaline anxiety can get those tasks crossed off the list. When you focus on a certain detail like the negative aspects of anxiety, if that is what you pay attention to, then your narrative has a negative lens.

Challenge the narrative and build awareness of the story you are telling yourself. Stories can foster anxiety, fear, sadness, anger, and frustration and can significantly impact your happiness. When you feel yourself getting stuck and thoughts become excessive or obsessive, this is your opportunity to tell yourself to let the story go. It is unhelpful and causing harm. Doing so takes practice. The more you let go, the easier it will be the next time. Perceiving someone being rude is a great way to practice letting go. Do not match their rudeness; let go of their rudeness and be kind.

Thinking Habits

Anxiety can cause you to develop odd thinking habits such as stubbornness, perfection, and excessive and obsessive thoughts. Stubbornness with control looks like when you tell yourself you cannot do something because of anxiety, such as "I can never make a penalty shot because I have anxiety," even if you are the best player on the team. Perfection is a way to seek control by making sure everything lines up in place and performs the way it should in our head. However, it's not realistic. Perfection is rare and mistakes are inevitable. Excessive and obsessive thoughts feed our anxiety like gas to a fire. They trigger each other, causing the next thought to spring up and make us feel bad.

You can break these thought habits by letting them go. You do not need to be stubborn and hold on to your anxiety. You can let go of perfection because to be perfect is boring; be you, knowing that your flaws are unique. Let go of what people think and let that anxiety narrative be someone else's story. Let go of what you cannot control. Be responsible for what you can, though, and be kind. Letting go frees us from the constraints and chains that anxiety creates. When you let go of all these anxious thinking habits, you will make space for the things that matter the most. You will be able to be your true self who is perfectly imperfect!

REAL TALK

Sam was a very artistic student who always wore different glasses. Sam had a learning disability of being dyslexic; reading and spelling were tough for him, but he was great at math. Sam told me he would stress out when the teacher would call on him to read aloud. "I stress out that I am going to mix the words up or not be able to read them; my hands shake, and I feel hot all over. What do I do?" I took a deep breath and smiled, saying, "Sam, have you told your teachers how you feel?" Sam looked at me like I had 10 heads. "Five to fifteen percent of children and adults have dyslexia and are successful. We need to find a way for it to not define you. Because it is part of you, and it makes you great at word scrambles." Sam laughed, "If only my AP test was a word scramble." I talked to Sam about how letting others in and sharing your anxiety and feelings is a strength. Sam disclosed how hard it was to keep his secret and when he didn't know how to spell something, he would tell people he was too tired. I said, "That sounds exhausting to hide yourself and cover up how you are struggling." He said, "You are right, I am dyslexic, and it is what it is. I need to just let it go."

Like Sam, we all have something we hide, something we shield from others. Once Sam was able to accept that being dyslexic did not make him less than, he was able to tell his teachers, who agreed to have him read when he raised his hand. Sam came into my office and was so excited. He said, "All my teachers were so cool about it, and no one looked at me weird."

Sometimes you build the narrative that things are worse than reality. When you let go, you embrace the freedom of whatever has been holding you back to be your awesome self.

Sweet Dreams

Often your brain is full of lists and busy thoughts, and you get caught up in what happened within your day. Sometimes it can feel as if you are reliving the day with judgment and seeing your mistakes on repeat. You are going to break that cycle with practice to support healthy sleep. Unlike other meditations you've done, you are going to do this one before bed. It is important that your phone and devices are put away and any blue lights are turned off. Recharge yourself each night by giving your brain space to be free from your to-do list and worries. Positive sleep hygiene will help you manage your anxiety. It will send a signal to your brain that it is time to wind down and let go of the day. Develop a routine like this where you give yourself time and space to let go of daily worries and stress.

1. Lie down and get very comfortable.
2. Adjust your body and feel how it is feeling. Feel that it is tired and needs to be recharged.
3. Feel each part of your body, from your head on a pillow all the way to your feet on the bed.
4. When comfortable, close your eyes.
5. Take a deep breath in, count to three, and release.
6. Be aware of your breath and focus on your belly.
7. Place your hands on your chest, rubbing slowly up and down.
8. As you breathe in and out, feel your eyes getting heavy.
9. Relax your jaw and release it if it is clenching.
10. Feel your energy healing your body as you give it awareness and care.
11. Change is constant, and your body is taking care of you.
12. There is no right or wrong in this moment.
13. Breathe in calm and breathe out worry.
14. With each breath, release a worry.
15. Listen and hear light sounds of rain.

16. The rain is washing away your worry.

17. It is helping you let go of stress and guiding you to recharge with sleep and relaxation.

18. Take a deep breath in for yourself in this moment, and breathe out and let go of anything you need to in this moment.

19. Rest and recharge and let go of all the things that are holding you back and not keeping you present.

Fan Club

In business there is a rule of 10-80-10: When you have an idea, or want to make a change, a way to improve how things are done, a new product, an invention, all the way to changing your personal style, there will be 10 percent who hate it, 80 percent who will be indifferent, and 10 percent who will be in your fan club. Your anxiety often listens to the 10 percent who hate it and the 80 percent who do not care either way. You are going to let go of the first 10 percent because, like Taylor Swift taught us, there may be people who think negatively, but you can shake it off.

1. First, you are going to take those song lyrics and create an affirmation.
    Here is an example:
    Regardless of what people say, I am awesome.
    Haters challenge me to stand taller.
    I am going to let go of what others think about me.
    I am going to trust my fan club to cheer me on.

2. Make your own:

    _____

    _____

    _____

    _____

3. Be vulnerable and tell yourself why you hold on to or listen to hurtful messages. Journal below and just let your thoughts come naturally.

_____

_____

_____

_____

_____

4. How will you open yourself to hear and listen to your fan club? Often, we filter out the compliments, accolades, and awards. What do you need to hear them?

_____

_____

_____

_____

_____

Spark Joy!

Take the KonMari Method and use it for your thoughts. Evaluate the thoughts in your life: What sparks joy and what is not helpful? Building awareness of the things you carry and hold on to is important. The past can hold you back and weigh you down. Consider things like the belongings you collect—clothes, books, papers, and sentimental possessions. Not everything you keep likely brings you joy and inspires you to be yourself.

→ When the negative thoughts from the past come up, let them go; they do not spark joy.

→ When you are thinking about what someone thinks about you, let it go; it does not spark joy.

→ When you think of the messages you have heard that are hurtful, let them go; they do not spark joy.

→ When you feel anxiety surging, let go of the fear; it does not spark joy.

→ When the tiny voice in your head tells you that you are not enough, let it go; it does not spark joy.

Reflect: What areas do you need to let go of in order to let in the light of joy?

_____

_____

Let it Go!

The song "Let It Go!" is sung in 41 different languages, sold more than 10.9 million copies in 2014, and has more than a billion views on YouTube. Embrace your inner Elsa and free yourself from every narrative, every person, every negative thought!

Reflect:

What do you need to not hold back?

_____

What do you need to let go of that someone has said to you?

_____

What is something that bothered you but you kept hidden?

_____

What is a fear you need to let go of?

_____

What can you do if you let your fear go?

_____

If you let go, what will you be free of?

_____

YOU'VE GOT THIS!

"When I let go of what I am, I become what I might be."

— Laozi

Anxiety can have you feeling like you are stuck in quicksand. Grab a rope and let go of your fear. Open yourself to the endless possibilities through mindfulness.

Ten Ways to Let Go!

1. When negative or painful thoughts come, challenge them with an affirmation.
2. Be kind to yourself and allow mistakes, which help you learn.
3. Practice mindfulness as a daily practice. Even two minutes a day makes a difference!
4. When negative emotions show up, do not push them away; invite them in and give them a hug.
5. Emotional and physical boundaries can help you create healthy distance, which allows for a new perspective. (You cannot see the forest through the trees; get on the balcony if you need a new view.)
6. Focus on your work and your contribution to the world. You are not responsible for others not showing up (unless you forgot to pick them up).
7. Accept people for who they are, not necessarily who you thought they were.
8. Say you're sorry: Apologize for when you were not your best; it makes you taller. Accept that other people may not always apologize when they should.
9. Expectations can lead to disappointment; do not only invest in the outcome, invest in the journey.
10. Find humor in everything possible; you will have great stories to tell.

Check Yourself

Anxiety and your busy life can make time and space feel burdensome. You may feel like you need to cross a certain number of items off your to-do list. Your brain can feel on autopilot when you are doing things. You are there but not really there. Jon Kabat-Zinn suggests that a great way to check yourself is when you are in the shower. Are you really in the shower or is your history test or project in the shower with you? Is the fight that you had with a friend in the shower, too? One way for you to check yourself is to develop awareness of where you are in the moment.

Let's practice checking in and letting go. You can do this when you feel yourself drifting somewhere else or when something else is with you that you don't feel belongs with you in that moment (like in the shower!). Check in with yourself and then tell yourself to let go of what does not belong.

Checking-in Questions

→ Where are you?

→ Where should you be?

→ Who is with you?

→ What are they saying to you?

→ What are you doing in this moment now?

Give Yourself Permission to "Let Go!"

→ Intrusive thought—Let Go!

→ To-do list—Let Go!

→ Past memory playing over and over—Let Go!

→ Worrying about tomorrow—Let Go!

→ Feeling like you need to do something different—Let Go!

One thing you can tell yourself is, "I do not need to worry about that in this moment." This can help you transition to being mindful without dismissing whatever you are thinking about as not important. You can always return to your thoughts at another time when you have the space and time to address them.

Helpful Not Helpful

Reflecting on what is helpful to you and what is not is a great way to evaluate your thoughts. This way you can let go of what is not helpful and focus on what is helpful. When your thoughts come, use the Helpful Not Helpful Meter to guide and help you sort out your thoughts.

Helpful Not Helpful Meter

→ **Is this thought helping me?**

→ **Is this thought making me feel bad about myself or others?**

→ **Is this thought something I can give attention to later?**

→ **Is this thought adding to my anxiety?**

Generate three different thoughts that help you.
Example: This is hard, and you can do it.

_____

_____

_____

Write three automatic anxiety thoughts that show up regularly.
Example: I can't do this.

_____

_____

_____

Letting go will help you stay present and focus on what is in front of you.

MINDFUL MOMENT

Letting go is the path to freedom from anxiety! Anxiety and worry thoughts follow the same path over and over again and create an anxiety spiral, a wheel of insecurity and doubt. Letting go will release these unhelpful thoughts and feelings and break that cycle. Just like falling asleep and giving in to peace and calm, you can use that skill to help yourself open up to a new path. You tend to hold on to things that keep you stuck out of fear. Remind yourself that transitions are part of your life and that you have been successful many times in the past. You have transitioned through teachers, friends, your favorite sneakers, etc. When you mindfully let go, you can open the next opportunity for growth, learning, and understanding. Your relationships will grow stronger as you release the burden of all the baggage you have been carrying. Letting go will keep the moments, relationships, and thoughts that spark joy in your life. Consider checking in with yourself throughout the day. Jon Kabat-Zinn suggests, "In letting go of wanting something special to occur, maybe we realize that something special is already occurring." Mindfulness is a practice, and the attitude of letting go will open you to the present moment that is special. This moment right now is unique and will never happen exactly the same again; enjoy the present and stay mindful.

POSITIVE VIBES

Anxiety can weigh you down with thoughts, feelings, safety behaviors, etc. Remember to let go and be present with those you care about and matter to you. When you are feeling overwhelmed and worry is loud in your mind, release your worries and let go of the things you cannot control.

YOUR TAKEAWAYS

→ Anxiety can cause a push and pull within you. You can push away hard feelings, dismiss positive moments, and grasp on to thought and experiences that hold you back.

→ When you let go, you free yourself from this burden and open yourself up to new ideas and positivity.

→ Letting go of the narratives that you tell yourself will help you stay present and pay attention to what matters the most.

→ Keep what sparks joy in your life and let go of all the fears, thoughts, and possessions that are holding you back.

→ Checking in with yourself will support letting go of your fear and keep you tuned in to what you need in this moment.

Idea Questions

→ How will you practice letting go this week?

→ How will you embrace releasing yourself from what you have been holding on to that is keeping you from moving forward?

→ What is one strategy you will use to practice letting go?

→ What is something that you realized you need to let go of after reading this chapter?

CHAPTER NINE

MINDFUL PATH FORWARD

You've arrived at the last chapter, and yet it is just the beginning of your amazing journey to living mindfully! As you continue your mindful path forward, my hope is that you take away two things:

1. Mindfulness is a practice, and the more you practice, the stronger you will become.

2. Anxiety does not vanish; it is managed with tools and time.

Are you as excited as I am about embarking on this mindful path forward? It really is the beginning of you taking all that you have learned and strengthening your mindfulness practice as you develop your own practice of the seven attitudes of mindfulness: beginner's mind, non-judging, acceptance, patience, trust, non-striving, and letting go. You will use these skills to manage your anxiety and stress as challenges arise in your life and relationships. In this chapter, you will build a prevention and maintenance plan that works uniquely for you. When you find yourself struggling, remember you are worth the investment! Life is all about learning, and to be successful, we often need to ask for help. You have a cadre of people in your life who are your network; lean in!

JUST THE FIRST STEP

Remember, you are a work in progress! Just like your teeth that you brush, your mental wellness needs a hygiene plan. Mental hygiene is what you do for your mental state, such as activities and strategies that help you foster positive mental health. It helps you develop and sustain relationships and helps you make constructive changes in your life. What does a mental wellness hygiene plan look like? It looks unique to everyone, and there is no right or wrong way to practice. You may want to set an intention for the day with one of the You've Got This or Positive Vibes sections. You may also want to pick one exercise and focus on that for the week to really dive into it. When you do things repetitively, you go deeper and notice or understand things you did not see before.

Mindfulness is available to you in every moment. When you need to lean in and stay in the moment, take the opportunity to use the skills you have developed throughout this workbook. Jon Kabat-Zinn practices mindfulness every day; that is why he is a master! Most people are novices, learning the concepts and building their foundational skills. In fact, mastering something like mindfulness is a lifelong path and process, as you are always developing and evolving. Think of yourself two years ago and how much you have learned; now, think of yourself before you picked up this workbook. You have come a long way, and each step forward led to positive change as you continue to build your library of knowledge.

There are a few books in my life I reread every few years to deepen my understanding. Hopefully, this is one of those books you can refer back to. Affirmations are great to keep in rotation, motivating and inspiring you to be your best self. Revisit your favorite ones, take a picture with your phone, and save it. This way, no matter where you are, you can reflect and regulate yourself. Return to your favorite exercises when you need to strengthen a skill or remind yourself of a tool you want to refresh yourself on using. You may want to go back and mark the page or highlight the ones that echoed with your learning the most.

Progress Check

In chapter 2, you took the 10-question Reality Check quiz where you were evaluating if your vision was 20/20 with regard to your anxiety. Don't go back and look at your responses just yet. For now, you are going to pivot and reflect on personal growth and areas where you may need further development. For the statements below, think about the last two weeks and how you were feeling, without judgment. Mark your frequency selection in the boxes with a check, a star, or an X. Simply record and observe the answers that come to mind. There is no need to analyze them.

QUESTION	ALWAYS	OFTEN	SOMETIMES	RARELY	NEVER
I worry about a lot of different things.					
I am easily annoyed or grouchy.					
It is hard for me to relax.					
I feel nervous, anxious, or impatient.					
I am afraid something bad will happen.					
It is hard for me to sit still without fidgeting.					
I cannot control my worried thoughts.					
I have a hard time focusing and feel distracted.					
I have a hard time getting to sleep or staying asleep.					
I avoid doing things that make me nervous.					

Reflect: Go back and look at your answers from chapter 2 (page 24) for reflection, without judgment or shame. You are letting go of those emotions through this exercise.

Beginner's mind: You see your answers with openness.

Non-judging: You see your answers for what they are and observe them.

Acceptance: You accept the answers and embrace your path forward.

Patience: You have patience with yourself as change takes time.

Trust: You have developed trust in yourself that will help you as you go forward.

Non-striving: You are developing a mindfulness practice that will help you reach your goals.

Letting go: You let go of judgment and just witness room for growth.

YOU'VE GOT THIS!

Your mindfulness practice is unique to you; take what you need, take what works, and let go of what doesn't. Leave the past in the past, and venture forward with optimism as your guide. The world is waiting and ready for your greatness!

FINDING WHAT WORKS FOR YOU

Schedules vary, and life happens to be messy, busy, and unpredictable. Creating a sustainable plan to manage your anxiety and grow your mindfulness practice will help set you up for success. You feed your body every day, and your mind also needs to be fed self-care and self-compassion. Be intentional that you do not make yourself or your mental wellness your last priority, or the last thing you cross off that to-do list. Be intentional about what works for you. When you went through the exercises in this book, there were exercises that were probably major wins for you and some that were not as much. The exercises that taught you a new perspective or gave you an aha moment may continue to do so, or else maybe you find some that didn't so much have an impact before now suddenly do. This is the benefit of returning to the exercises and continuing the progression to mindfulness.

Build mental wellness into your day, not unlike getting dressed and brushing your teeth. If you are like me, you prioritize charging your phone, and do it without thinking (before bed or first thing in the morning while getting ready). Having a full battery sets me up for success, and we want to do this for your mental wellness as well. You need to recharge your personal battery just as easily as you do your phone. Each morning, set an intention, read an affirmation, etc., to support your overall mental health for the day. Throughout the day, check in with yourself and see where you are by being present, evaluate what you need to accept, develop patience with yourself, or learn to trust yourself. Before bed, reflect on what went well and observe the areas that needed a hug. Let go of the shame and encourage yourself to keep on the path of mindfulness one step at a time.

High five for diving in and building your mindfulness toolbox and your mindfulness practice! It has been a journey through reflection and challenging yourself to learn new things. Each chapter you learned a new mindfulness attitude and completed exercises giving you strategies and tools for your future. You have pushed yourself emotionally and identified where anxiety is present in your life. You have also developed awareness of what you need to manage your anxiety. The energy and time you have given is always worth the investment when it comes to mental wellness and your health. Use the exercises in this workbook as you go forward to keep progressing, and if you feel stuck, use your mindfulness skills to let go. Continue on this path of investment and personal growth and keep your beginner's mind handy to see clearly with fresh eyes. Finally, make a game plan!

Game Plan

Everyone needs a mental hygiene game plan! In this exercise you will map out your mental hygiene and mindfulness game plan. You will be purposeful in setting your intentions throughout the week. Below is a sample game plan with six key mental wellness goals: mindfulness, personal care (this is anything you do to take care of your body), water (setting a goal of how much to drink), exercise, healthy snacks, and practicing your own affirmation. You can modify to fit your mental wellness needs and create your own. Celebrating your commitment with stars and X's will positively reinforce your goals! It will also help you reflect on areas of your life that need more attention. You may be great at saying "no" to chips and choosing a healthy snack instead, but you might need to practice your affirmation more. Certain goals and intentions come easier to you than others, and you have to work a little harder at them. Your game plan will help you identify the areas that you can celebrate and develop.

WELLNESS GOAL	MON	TUES	WED	THURS	FRI
Mindfulness					
Personal care					
Water					
Exercise					
Healthy snacks					
Practice affirmation					

Affirmation for the week: _____

KEEP UP THE MOMENTUM

Anxiety does not have a cure; however, relief and management are possible. You are ahead of the curve just by reading this workbook! It takes most people eight to nine years to seek help with their anxiety, as recognizing stress being out of bounds is difficult. Coping with anxiety is key! Use your mindfulness skills to accept it as part of you. If you had a broken arm, you would say, without judgment, "I have a broken arm." Anxiety is the same thing; it is what it is. The difference between a broken arm and your anxiety is you can use your patience and trust in yourself to help manage your anxiety. Pay attention to your triggers and when your stress and anxiety are pushing the out-of-bounds line. And when your anxiety gets out of bounds, observe the pattern or patterns. What do you notice? What was happening before your anxiety-out-of-bounds alarm went off? How are you reacting in this moment? Stay curious and use your beginner's mind to see the pattern. If you have a stacked week of things to do, deadlines, and turbulence in your relationships, take a step back and make a game plan.

Ellen DeGeneres said, "When you take risks, you learn that there will be times when you succeed and there will be times when you fail, and both are equally important." Managing your anxiety is a positive risk. You have to experiment to know what will work for you in this moment. Your anxiety today may be different from yesterday, and therefore needs a different plan of action. Each day there are different variables, such as eating, exercising, and sleeping. In order to figure out what you need, there may be a few missteps. Take them as learning opportunities, because when you fail, you are figuring out what you need. Also, when you realize something did not work, you know that is not your go-to strategy. Your go-to strategy will come to you through trial and error. You will try one thing and realize you actually liked something else better. Congratulations for figuring it out and using your problem-solving skills.

The work will go on even after this book. You have developed strategies and a game plan to help you along the way forward. Investing in your personal welfare and growth takes effort. The work that you invest will surely deliver a positive return. One way to keep going and keep the momentum is to have an accountability partner. Having someone in your life who is also practicing mindfulness with you will help keep you on track. There are times when you will quit on yourself, procrastinate, or even avoid a situation that you know will help you. You may tell yourself you will do it tomorrow, and tomorrow never seems to come. Having an accountability partner removes those barriers and holds you accountable for today. They keep you on track, and when you feel like quitting, you will follow through because someone else is counting on you.

WHAT TO DO IF YOU'RE STILL STRUGGLING

Life is filled with challenges, bumps, twists, and laughter. Managing your anxiety is a bit the same, certainly uncertain. As you keep going on your mindful path forward, be mindful that there are many avenues to manage your anxiety and emotions.

Talk Therapy

Talk therapy (also referred to as psychotherapy) is a great way to manage your anxiety. Just what it sounds like, talk therapy is when you talk with a therapist and strategize on how to support your overall wellness emotionally. The goal is to identify issues that are causing you stress in your life and even your relationships.

Telehealth/Teletherapy

Telehealth/teletherapy is talk therapy over a virtual platform or phone. Using technology adds flexibility to receiving services, is convenient for your schedule, and reduces any time commuting, as you are just one link or click away from support.

Cognitive Behavioral Therapy (CBT)

Cognitive behavioral therapy (CBT) helps build awareness to negative thought cycles. You learned several cognitive distortions in this book. CBT helps you change your thought patterns and identify the triggers. You may want to have multiple modalities to support your anxiety and mental wellness.

I always encourage people to therapy shop to find a therapist. No matter how well someone is trained or how many years the therapist has been providing therapy, if you and the therapist do not click, then there will be little growth. You have to find someone who you feel comfortable with to dive into the hard work. Go to a therapist a few times before moving on; you need to give your best and keep your beginner's mind sharp by being open. Disclaimer: as a therapist, I want what's best for you, and if that is not me, it's okay. There is a therapist for everyone, and I am not for everyone.

Asking for help is key! Asking for help doing the dishes may seem easier than asking for help related to your emotions. Emotions are harder to gauge, and you may struggle to recognize that you are having a difficult time until you feel like you are drowning. Check in with yourself regularly to monitor where your anxiety level lands. Your anxiety can build fear of asking for help; you may even feel shame. Let go of any shame and normalize that asking for help is part of your life.

While mindfulness has been around for more than 2,500 years, it has only recently come to the main stage of society. It is important to remember that building mindfulness takes time. Use the meditations in this book or find one you like online or through an application at the end of this book (page 168). You can build on the attitudes on mindfulness as you need them. You may want to focus on one or apply each one to your day. If you don't find what you need as you continue forward on your path to mindfulness, remember that there are many resources out there that are available to you: online classes, applications for your devices, cards, calendars, etc.

Asking for Help

Asking for emotional support can feel uncomfortable and even complicated at times. You may feel anxious, scared, judged, and minimized. Vulnerability takes strength, and asking for help shows how strong you are. Successful people ask for help, ask questions, and lean on their support team. Consider your network of family, friends, school staff, and other amazing adults in your life, like a coach, mentor, minister, etc. Approach someone who you feel is reliable, trustworthy, and honest. Tell the person you have identified about how you feel, what is being impacted, what you have tried, and what you need from them to help you. You can write it down if you feel like it will be difficult to say out loud. If it feels more comfortable, bring a friend for support. When talking about your feelings and emotions, be honest. Seeking help is the first step to a solution, and the person you are seeking support and help from needs all the facts.

STATEMENT	EXAMPLE	YOUR ANSWER
Recently I have been feeling:	Really anxious and my stomach hurts most days.	
What is being impacted:	I am having a hard time sleeping and concentrating.	
I have tried:	Meditating, talking with friends, and deep breathing.	
I need you to:	Help me talk to my teacher, because when they call on me my anxiety is at 100.	

Congratulate yourself on prioritizing your mental wellness—asking for help shows strength and courage!

Learn new things, ask questions, and stay courageous!

YOUR TAKEAWAYS

"Don't dwell on what went wrong. Instead, focus on what to do next. Spend your energy moving forward together towards an answer."

— Denis Waitley

→ Mindfulness is a practice, and your practice is unique to you. The more you integrate mindfulness into your daily life, the stronger your practice will become.

→ Anxiety comes and goes, but it never disappears. You have learned new tools and strategies, and with practice managing your anxiety will take less effort.

→ Finding what works for you is key. Building your own system, your own schedule, will help keep you accountable. If you fall, just regroup and pick up where you left off.

→ Applications, websites, your support network, trusted adults, and mental health professionals are there for support and learning.

Idea Questions

→ What is one success from your progress check that you want to high-five yourself for?

→ What is one strategy you will use to practice mindfulness?

→ What is something that you realized you need after reading this chapter?

RESOURCES

Applications

Calm

Features more than 100 million downloads of music, videos, stories, audio, and nature sounds and scenes to support relaxation, studying, and working. If you are looking for mindfulness tools in one place that support sleep, meditation, relaxation, and mindfulness, this is the app for you.

Daylio Journal

Recommended by several therapists, this app offers a unique way to track your happiness and mood. Offering a digital bullet journal, you can track your self-care and self-improvement and monitor your overall well-being.

Insight Timer

Helping you build your mindfulness practice that meets your scheduling needs, this app features guided meditations and talks by experts. The app uses celebrity artists for the songs and is fun to connect with.

Stop, Breathe & Think

We all need a pause to fit mindfulness in our lives. This app can fit into your schedule with breathing exercises, yoga, guided meditation, and journaling.

Books & Tools

Mindful Moments: Guided Exercises and Mantras for Kids
The everyday mindfulness exercises on these cards provide empowering mantras to increase emotional intelligence, improve focus, build resilience, reduce anxiety, and help children feel calmer and more connected to the world around them. I use them even as an adult.
BoundlessBlooms.world

Affirmators!
Whimsical and fun, the 50 Affirmation Card decks help you help yourself. There are many to choose from, and they are great to keep on your desk or in a bag when you need to be reminded of a daily intention. Conceived and written by Suzi Barrett and illustrated by Naomi Sloman.
KnockKnockStuff.com

How to Train a Wild Elephant: And Other Adventures in Mindfulness
Written by Jan Chozen Bays (Boulder, Colo.: Shambhala Press, 2011). Tangible mindfulness practices that you can easily turn into daily habits.

The Self-Compassion Workbook for Teens: Mindfulness and Compassion Skills to Overcome Self-Criticism and Embrace Who You Are
Written By Karen Bluth, PhD (Oakland, Cal.: Instant Help, 2017).

Mindfulness for Teens in 10 Minutes a Day: Exercises to Feel Calm, Stay Focused & Be Your Best Self
Written by Jennie Marie Battistin, MA, LMFT (Emeryville, Cal.: Rockridge Press, 2019). The author provides 10-minute exercises to develop a sense of calm, clear focus, and reconnection to be your best self. This book normalizes life's stressors and brings in mindfulness to the front, taking control of being overwhelmed.

Hotlines & Websites

Erika's Lighthouse: ErikasLighthouse.org
Erika's Lighthouse offers a community to "Get Depression Out of the Dark," with a wide array of resources for teens, parents, and educators on teen depression with toolkits, activities, and more!

TEEN LINE: 800-852-8336 or text TEEN to 839863
If you want to talk with someone who understands, such as another teen, you can text or call. Their goal is unique, offering a teen-to-teen point of view. The hours vary on texting and calling to provide support, education, and resources. Reach out for help before a problem becomes a crisis: TeenlineOnline.org.

The Trevor Project: 866-488-7386 or text START to 678-678
The Trevor Project operates the only nationwide 24/7 helpline supporting teens in crisis and providing suicide prevention for lesbian, gay, bisexual, transgender, and questioning (LGBTQ) youth. The Trevor Helpline provides a community approach supporting parents, family members, and friends: TheTrevorProject.org.

National Suicide Prevention Lifeline: 800-273-8255
The Lifeline provides 24/7 suicide prevention support. All services are at no cost and confidential. If you or a loved one is in crisis or needs a resource, they have a dedicated team to support and help prevent suicide: SuicidePreventionLifeline.org/.

National Alliance on Mental Illness: 1-800-950-NAMI (6264) or text NAMI to 741-741
The NAMI HelpLine offers education, support, and resources for anyone living or supporting someone with a mental health condition. All services and information are at no cost. Uniquely, they offer peer support and information to mental health practitioners: Nami.org.

REFERENCES

Adamski, Carol. "Living in Gratitude: Self-Acceptance Leads to Higher Happiness." Gratitude Habitat. September 15, 2018. Gratitudehabitat .com/2018/09/living-in-gratitude-self-acceptance-leads-to -higher-happiness/.

"Any Anxiety Disorder." National Institute of Mental Health, Last modified November 2017. Nimh.nih.gov/health/statistics/any-anxiety-disorder. shtml#:~:text=An%20estimated%2031.9%25%20of%20adolescents, than%20for%20males%20(26.1%25).

Brannen, Karen. "How Hugging Promotes Well-Being." LeadingAge. January 4, 2014. Leadingage.org/magazine/januaryfebruary-2014/ embraceable-you-how-hugging-promotes-well-being.

Cardaciotto, LeeAnn, James D. Herbert, Evan M. Forman, Ethan Moitra, and Victoria Farrow. "The Assessment of Present-Moment Awareness and Acceptance: The Philadelphia Mindfulness Scale." *SAGE Journals* 15, no. 2 (June 2008): 204-223. Greatergood.berkeley.edu/images/ uploads/Cardaciotto-Mindfulness_on_Present_Moment_Awareness _and_Acceptance.pdf.

Carr, Sam. "How Many Ads Do We See a Day? 2021 Daily Ad Exposure Revealed!" PPC Protect. February 15, 2021. Ppcprotect.com/how-many -ads-do-we-see-a-day/#:~:text=Fast%20forward%20to%202021% 2C%20and,10%2C000%20ads%20every%20single%20day.

Cohen, Sheldon, Denise Janicki-Deverts, Ronald B. Turner, et al. "Does Hugging Provide Stress-Buffering Social Support?" *Psychological Science 26*, no. 2 (December 2014): 135-147. Journals.sagepub.com /doi/abs/10.1177/0956797614559284.

Cox, Elizabeth. "What Is Imposter Syndrome and How Can You Combat It?" YouTube, TED-Ed. August 28, 2018. Youtube.com/watch?v =ZQUxL4Jm1Lo.

"The Dao De Jing." Angelfire.com/md2/timewarp/daodejing.html.

"Daoism." Encyclopedia. Britannica. Britannica.com/topic/Daoism.

"Donald Glover." En.wikipedia.org/wiki/Donald_Glover.

"Eating Mindfully for Teens: A Workbook to Help You Make Healthy Choices, End Emotional Eating & Feel Great Interview." *Eating Disorders Catalogue*. October 1, 2019. Edcatalogue.com/ eating-mindfully -teens-workbook-help-make-healthy-choices-end-emotional -eating-feel-great-interview/.

"Ford Factory Workers Get 40-Hour Week." History.com. Last modified April 29, 2020. History.com/this-day-in-history/ford-factory-workers -get-40-hour-week.

"Frozen Lyrics." Google.com/search?q=frozen%2Blyrics&rlz=1C1CHBD _enUS910US910&oq=frozen%2Blyr&aqs=chrome.0.0l3j69i57j0l6 .3753j0j7&sourceid=chrome&ie=UTF-8.

Galderisi, Silvana, Andreas Heinz, Marianne Kastrup, Julian Beezhold, and Norman Sartorius. "Toward a New Definition of Mental Health." *World Psychiatry* 14, no. 2 (June 2015): 231-233. Online Library, June 4, 2015, onlinelibrary.wiley.com/doi/full/10.1002/wps.20231.

Hauck, Carley "The Power of Letting Go." *Mindful*. October 16, 2017, Mindful.org/power-letting-go/.

Herbert, James D., and Lynn L. Brandsma. "Understanding and Enhancing Psychological Acceptance." Une.edu/sites/default /files/herbertbrandsma_mindfulness.pdf.

"How Many Google Searches Per Day Are There?" Skai. February 25, 2019. Skai.io/monday-morning-metrics-daily-searches-on-google-and -other-google-facts/.

"Jon Kabat-Zinn Quotes About Acceptance." A-Z Quotes. Azquotes.com /author/8354-Jon_Kabat_Zinn/tag/acceptance.

Kee, Ying Hwa, Khin Maung Aye, Raisyad Ferozd, and Chunxiao Li. "Effects of a Brief Strange Loop Task on Immediate Word Length Comparison: A Mindfulness Study on Non-Striving." *Frontiers in Psychology*. October 11, 2019. Frontiersin.org/articles/10.3389/fpsyg.2019.02314/full.

Kondo, Marie. "About KonMari: The Official Website of Marie Kondo." Konmari.com.

Kunz, Rowan. "What Hugh Jackman Taught Me About the Art of Not-Doing." Rowankunz.com/the-art-of-not-doing/.

Langeveld, Irene. "Why Grounding Can Be Difficult Sometimes + What To Do About It." Mindbodygreen. Last modified February 24, 2020. Mindbodygreen.com/0-17987/why-grounding-is-difficult-for-highly -sensitive-people-what-to-do-about-it.html#:~:text=Being%20 %22grounded%22%20means%20that%20you,thrown%20off%20 balance%20very%20quickly.

"Let It Go." Accessed April 18, 2021. En.wikipedia.org/wiki/Let_It_Go.

Mind, Spiritual. "Beginner's Mind - Jon Kabat-Zinn - Mindfulness - Includes Music." YouTube. January 23, 2018. Youtube.com/watch?v =Vbok6_PgMKs.

"Mindfulness Definition: What Is Mindfulness." Greater Good. Greatergood .berkeley.edu/topic/mindfulness/definition#:~:text=Mindfulness %20means%20maintaining%20a%20moment,through%20a %20gentle%2C%20nurturing%20lens.&text=When%20we %20practice%20mindfulness%2C%20our,past%20or%20imagining %20the%20future.

"Mindfulness Meditation About the Author." Guided Mindfulness Meditation Practices with Jon Kabat-Zinn. Mindfulnesscds.com/pages /about-the-author.

"NYU Study Examines Top High School Students' Stress and Coping Mechanisms." NYU. Last modified August 11, 2015. Nyu.edu/about/ news-publications/news/2015/august/nyu-study-examines-top -high-school-students-stress-and-coping-mechanisms.html.

"Pareto Principle." Accessed April 11, 2021. En.wikipedia.org/wiki/Pareto _principle.

Powell, Alvin. "When Science Meets Mindfulness." *Harvard Gazette*. April 9, 2018. News.harvard.edu/gazette/story/2018/04/harvard-researchers -study-how-mindfulness-may-change-the-brain-in-depressed -patients/.

Raymond, Les, and Sara Raymond. The Mindful Movement. Themindfulmovement.com/.

Skelly, Samantha. "Trusting Yourself with Food." Recovery.org. June 16, 2019. Recovery.org/pro/articles/trusting-yourself-with-food/.

Society for Neuroscience. "Dyslexia: What Brain Research Reveals About Reading." LD Online. Ldonline.org/article/10784/#:~:text=A %20staggering%205%20to%2015,intelligent%20he%20or %20she%20is.

Steenbarger, Brett. "Moving the Body, Transforming the Mind: The Psychology of Dance." *Forbes Magazine*. October 31, 2020. Forbes.com /sites/brettsteenbarger/2020/10/31/moving-the-body-transforming -the-mind-the-psychology-of-dance/?sh=40f6dab13ef7.

Vital, Anna. "Counting the People Your Life Impacts—Infographic." Adioma. April 29, 2013. Blog.adioma.com/counting-the-people -you-impact-infographic/#:~:text=On%20average%20we %20live%20for,3%20x%20365.24%20%3D%2080%2C000 %20people.

Walter, Ekaterina. "30 Powerful Quotes on Failure." *Forbes Magazine*. December 30, 2013. Forbes.com/sites/ekaterinawalter/2013/12/30/30-powerful-quotes-on-failure/?sh=477d6ace24bd.

Whalley, Matthew. "Cognitive Distortions: Unhelpful Thinking Habits." *Psychology Tools*, March 18, 2019. Psychologytools.com/articles/unhelpful-thinking-styles-cognitive-distortions-in-cbt/.

"What Does Patience Is a Virtue Mean?" Writing Explained. Writingexplained.org/idiom-dictionary/patience-is-a-virtue.

"What Is Cognitive Behavioral Therapy?" American Psychological Association. Apa.org/ptsd-guideline/patients-and-families/cognitive-behavioral.

Zakashansky, Michele. "Practice Non-Striving." Amherst Mindfulness. May 11, 2016. Amherstmindfulness.com/single-post/2016/05/11/practice-nonstriving.

INDEX

ACKNOWLEDGMENTS

Writing a book is a surreal and privileged opportunity that I will always be forever grateful for. I am appreciative of every reader who challenged themselves with this workbook.

A very special thank-you to my editors Sean Newcott and Aric Dutelle, and Callisto Media for adding their geniuses. Jessica McKimmey Photography, thank you for chasing the light. Shout-out to my social media director Kimberly Iovine for teaching me the power of a hashtag.

To my amazing family, thank you for believing in me and making this sacrifice of time. Nathan, thank you for always joining my circus and proofreading my drafts. Kirin and Finnley, thank you for learning more about anxiety than you ever desired and cheering me on.

I am infinitely grateful for everyone's investment!

Group hug!

ABOUT THE AUTHOR

Sally Annjanece Stevens, LCSW, PPSC, MEd, is a social worker, speaker, author, and founder of Anchor Yourself Wellness. Sally's career in education began in Los Angeles County over a decade ago as a school social worker. Erika's Lighthouse named Sally educator of the year in 2020. Sally is also the author of *Social Anxiety Workbook for Teens: 10-Minute Methods to Reduce Stress and Gain Confidence*.

Sally is the proud mother of two children, Finnley (daughter) and Kirin (son), and a wife to Nathan (a chemistry teacher). Education is a passionate theme in their home, where mental health is talked about regularly and science experiments are encouraged. Readers can find out more about Sally at AnchorYourselfWellness.com or follow her on all social media platforms @anchoryourselfwellness.

Printed in the USA
CPSIA information can be obtained
at www.ICGtesting.com
CBHW060840010724
10682CB00001B/3